how2become

GCSE Religious Studies is Easy

www.How2Become.com

Orders: Please contact How2Become Ltd, Suite 14, 50 Churchill Square Business Centre, Kings Hill, Kent ME19 4YU.

You can order through Amazon.co.uk under ISBN 9781912370429, via the website www.How2Become.com, Gardners or Bertrams.

ISBN: 9781912370429

First published in 2018 by How2Become Ltd.

Copyright © 2018 How2Become.

All rights reserved. Apart from any permitted use under UK copyright law, no part of this publication may be reproduced or transmitted in any form or by any means, electronic or mechanical, including photocopying, recording, or any information, storage or retrieval system, without permission in writing from the publisher or under licence from the Copyright Licensing Agency Limited. Further details of such licenses (for reprographic reproduction) may be obtained from the Copyright Licensing Agency Ltd, Saffron House, 6-10 Kirby Street, London EC1N 8TS.

Typeset for How2Become Ltd by Gemma Butler.

Disclaimer

Every effort has been made to ensure that the information contained within this guide is accurate at the time of publication. How2Become Ltd is not responsible for anyone failing any part of any selection process as a result of the information contained within this guide. How2Become Ltd and their authors cannot accept any responsibility for any errors or omissions within this guide, however caused. No responsibility for loss or damage occasioned by any person acting, or refraining from action, as a result of the material in this publication can be accepted by How2Become Ltd.

The information within this guide does not represent the views of any third-party service or organisation.

As part of this product you have also received FREE access to online tests that will help you to pass your GCSEs.

To gain access, simply go to:

www.MyEducationalTests.co.uk

Get more products for passing any test at:

www.How2Become.com

Contents page

INTRODUCTION TO YOUR GUIDE ... 9
    What is Religious Studies? ... 10
    Contents of the Religious Studies GCSE Curriculum ... 11
    Assessment Objectives for Religious Studies GCSE ... 11
    Contents of this Book ... 14

UNIT 1: BELIEFS, TEACHINGS, AND PRACTICES

CHRISTIANITY AND CATHOLICISM ... 17
    What is Christianity? ... 18
    The Bible ... 18
    The Ten Commandments ... 20
    Key Differences Between Christianity and Catholic Christianity (Catholicism) ... 23
    The Core Beliefs of Christianity ... 25
    The Life of Jesus Christ ... 33
    Life, Death, and the Afterlife ... 35
    The Sacraments, Prayer, and Worship ... 37

ISLAM ... 43
    What is Islam? ... 44
    The Qur'an ... 45
    The Key Differences Between Sunni and Shi'a Muslims ... 46
    Core Principles of Islam ... 48
    The Nature of Allah ... 51
    The Life of the Prophet Muhammed ... 51
    Life, Death, and the Afterlife ... 52
    Muslim Worship and Festivals ... 52

JUDAISM 57
What is Judaism? 58
The Tenakh and Talmud 59
Core Beliefs in Judaism 61
The Key Differences Between Orthodox and Progressive Judaism 64
Life, Death, and the Afterlife 65
Sacred Places and Places of Worship 66
Festivals and Worship 66

UNIT 2: RELIGION IN PRACTICE

THE EXISTENCE OF GOD 69
The Design Argument 70
The First Cause Argument 72
The Existence of Miracles 73
Exam-Style Questions 75

RELIGION AND THE WORLD 77
Religion and the Environment 78
Religion and the Universe 79
Religion, Abortion, and Euthanasia 82
Exam-Style Questions 86

RELIGION AND RELATIONSHIPS 87
Religion, Sex, and Sexuality 88
Religion and Contraception 90
Religion, Marriage, and Divorce 92
Exam-Style Questions 96

RELIGION, WAR, AND PEACE **97**
   Religion and War *98*
   Religion and Weapons of Mass Destruction (WMDs) *100*
   Exam-Style Questions *102*

REVISION AND EXAM TIPS **103**
   Revision Timetables and Planning *104*
   How do I motivate myself? *107*
   Staying Focused *108*
   Avoid Cramming! *111*
   Conclusion *112*
   Exam Techniques and Preparation *113*
   What are Exams? *114*
   Types of Exam *115*
   The Tiers: Foundation and Higher *115*
   Exam Tips and Techniques *117*
   Planning and Timing Your Exam *128*
   Using Mock Exams and Practice Questions *129*
   Mark Schemes *133*
   Stress *138*
   Conclusion *143*

A FEW FINAL WORDS… **145**
REMEMBER – THE THREE Ps! **146**

INTRODUCTION TO YOUR GUIDE

Welcome to *GCSE Religious Studies is Easy*. In this guide, you'll learn everything you need in order to unlock your full potential in your Religious Studies GCSE. From the core beliefs of each faith and how religion interacts with the modern world, all the way to revision and exam tips, this guide has everything you need in order to improve your chances of success in GCSE Religious Studies.

Religious Studies can be incredibly difficult, especially if you aren't already familiar with the faiths and their practices. Each faith – and even denominations within a faith – has very different beliefs, both in terms of their core theology and the way they approach the world. This means that there's a lot to learn, but thankfully there are a plethora of ways to remember the important facts. This guide will walk you through everything that you need to know about faiths for your GCSE in Religious Studies.

What is Religious Studies?

As the name suggests, Religious Studies is the discipline of studying the different religions in the world. Within this field, there's a broad range of topics to cover. These include, but are not limited to:

1. The religious texts of a faith (e.g. the Bible, Qur'an, and Torah), interpretation of these texts, and their depictions of God and other prominent religious figures.

2. The core theological beliefs of a faith, such as the concept of God, nature of life and death, as well as reality and the universe.

3. The evidence that different religions use to substantiate their beliefs (e.g. miracles).

4. The way in which faiths deal with topics such as the existence of evil and revelation.

5. The moral stances of a religion on numerous issues (e.g. abortion, conflict, crime and punishment, and relationships).

These are all areas which are explored within the Religious Studies GCSE. As you work through this book, you'll learn about how different faiths interpret their own texts, what they believe about God's nature, how they prove God's existence, and how they approach philosophical and moral issues facing us in the modern world.

Contents of the Religious Studies GCSE Curriculum

The Religious Studies GCSE curriculum is split into two sections. The first, called "Beliefs, Teachings, and Practices", focuses on seven major world religions. These are:

- Buddhism;
- Christianity;
- Catholic Christianity (Catholicism);
- Hinduism;
- Islam;
- Judaism;
- Sikhism.

For each of these seven faiths, you will learn about their sacred texts, their core beliefs, and how they work within the modern world.

The second section of the Religious Studies GCSE curriculum is more focused on how the major religions approach philosophical, moral, and social issues within the world. These topics include:

- The Existence of God;
- Religion and Life;
- Religion and Relationships;
- Religion, War, and Peace;
- Religion and the Law;
- Religion and Human Rights.

Assessment Objectives for Religious Studies GCSE

The Religious Studies GCSE assesses the following two skills:

1. Your ability to demonstrate knowledge and understandings of religions, their beliefs, and impact on the world.
2. Your ability to evaluate a religion and elements of religion.

Simply put, these two skills translate to:

1. What you know (i.e. raw information that you've revised).
2. How well you can argue for or against an idea.

Questions which fall under the first skill will essentially test how much you've revised and can remember. A question of this kind might be:

> What are the names of the Five Pillars of Islam?

For this question, you don't need to evaluate, analyse, or form an argument. All you would need to do is list the Five Pillars of Islam:

1. Shahada: Faith.
2. Salah: Prayer.
3. Zakāt: Charity.
4. Sawm: Fasting.
5. Hajj: Pilgrimage.

So, you need to make sure that you learn everything in order to have the best chance of scoring highly for this kind of question.

The second kind of question will usually test your knowledge, but will go a step further and test your evaluative skills as well. You'll need a core foundation of knowledge in order to have an understanding of the topic, but you will also need to discuss the topics on an evaluative level.

Questions of this kind are similar to the following:

> 'It is more important for Catholics to give money to charity than it is for them to pray every day.'
>
> Evaluate this statement.

You can easily identify these questions by a number of factors:

1. They usually begin with a statement which is written as a quotation (i.e. it uses quotation marks).
2. Most questions of this kind will ask you to 'evaluate this statement'.
3. They tend to be accompanied by a lot of space to write your answer. This is because the examiner expects you to write much more than a single sentence!

INTRODUCTION TO YOUR GUIDE

4. These questions are usually worth a lot more marks than knowledge-based questions. Usually, these questions are worth at least 10 marks. In some cases, they might be worth even more!

So, these questions want you to do the following:

- Use your knowledge and understanding to present one point of view, usually by referring to the relevant teachings for the religion.

- Present a number of reasoned arguments for why you believe this point of view to be correct.

- Present a number of reasoned arguments for an opposing point of view.

- Come to a conclusion on why your original point of view is correct.

So, for the above question, your answer might consist of the following:

1. State that Catholics should give to charity because Jesus spent a lot of his ministry living among the poor.

2. Include a quote from the Bible, such as "Sell all that you possess and distribute it to the poor, and you shall have treasure in heaven." (Luke 18:22)

3. State that Catholics should strive to follow in Jesus' footsteps. Not only did he tell his followers to be charitable, but he also lived with minimal possessions rather than using his position to become wealthy.

4. Introduce a counter-argument, such as the fact that God will forgive all sins as long as you believe and pray to him.

5. Conclude that, even though God forgives all sins, he still wants us all to do our best to give to charity. Perhaps then, prayer and charity are equally important, and Catholics should devote equal attention to both.

For your answer, you might want to include more arguments and counter-arguments. If you can think of three major arguments for your position, and provide reasoning for each, you should be in a good position to score marks. Add two or three counter-arguments and you should have a strong answer on your hands.

For these questions, remember that you can't be right or wrong about the position you take. You're stating your opinion, and then you're backing it up with facts. For this reason, you still need to be accurate – if your argument is based on falsehoods, then it won't be considered a strong argument.

Essentially, these questions are less concerned with the position that you take, and are more focused on how you support it. This means you can take whatever stance you want, so long as it is relevant to the question and you support it properly.

Contents of this Book

Religion has played a fundamental role in the shaping of human civilisation. From the Greek and Roman faiths of antiquity, or the faiths which are still practised today, there are far too many faiths to talk about in a single book. Even within these faiths, there are *denominations* and *sects* which interpret religious texts differently. If we even attempted to discuss every single world religion in this book, this guide would take an extremely long time to read.

Instead, this book will focus on the following four faiths which are studied as part of Religious Studies GCSE:

- Christianity;
- Catholic Christianity (Catholicism);
- Islam;
- Judaism.

It's worth noting that Catholicism is a form of Christianity. This means that, while there are significant differences between Catholicism and other Christian denominations, they are both technically part of the same religion. This means that they share a lot of the same beliefs. For example, worshippers in both faiths believe that Jesus Christ is the son of God, and also that Jesus rose from the dead on Easter Sunday. Likewise, while Catholics and other types of Christians have differing codes of ethics, they agree on a number of issues.

The GCSE curriculum makes a distinction between Christianity and Catholic Christianity, so we have done so as well. However, we have decided to combine the chapters on Christianity and Catholicism. Major differences between Catholics and other types of Christian will be made clear at the beginning of the chapter on Christianity, and any minor differences will be highlighted where relevant.

After discussing the core beliefs of Christianity and Catholicism, we'll be shifting our focus to Saint Mark's Gospel: one of the four gospels featured in the Bible. In this guide, we'll be taking a look at the background of Mark's Gospel, as well as its content and interpretation.

After we've taken a look at Mark's Gospel, we'll move over from Christianity to Islam. Here, we'll take a look at what Islam is, what the core beliefs are, and also take a look at the Qur'an. We'll then shift our focus again to Judaism, discussing the same topics which we've looked at for Christianity and Islam. The study of these four faiths make up Unit 1: "Beliefs, Teachings, and Practices".

Once you've read and learned about the four faiths covered in this book, you'll be equipped to approach Unit 2: "Religion and the World". Unit 2 will encompass the following chapters:

- **The Existence of God** – This chapter will focus on arguments both for and against the existence of God, as well as the existence of miracles and other supernatural occurrences;

- **Religion and Life** – Here, we'll discuss how different faiths approach the concepts of life and death, and the nature of the universe. In addition, we'll take a look at how different religions approach moral questions involving life, such as our obligation to take care of the environment, abortion, and euthanasia;

- **Religion and Relationships** – In this chapter, you'll learn about how major religions approach topics such as sex, sexuality, marriage, divorce, and contraception;

- **Religion, War, and Peace** – This chapter will focus what each religion believes about conflict, as well as the role that they play in either creating or preventing conflict in the modern world.

For each of these topics, we'll take a look at what you need to know, as well as possible questions you might be faced with during your GCSE Religious Studies exam.

Finally, we'll be discussing some revision and exam tips to help you improve your chances of getting the highest possible grade in your Religious Studies GCSE.

UNIT 1: BELIEFS, TEACHINGS, AND PRACTICES

CHRISTIANITY AND CATHOLICISM

GCSE Religious Studies is Easy

In this chapter, we'll be taking a look at Christianity and Catholic Christianity. Here, you'll learn everything you need to know about the Christian faith. This will include the following topics:

1. What is Christianity?
2. The Bible.
3. The Ten Commandments.
4. Key Differences Between Christianity and Catholic Christianity.
5. The Core Beliefs of Christianity.
6. The Life of Jesus Christ.
7. Life, Death, and the Afterlife.
8. The Sacraments, Prayer, and Worship.

What is Christianity?

Christianity is the major religion based on the life of Jesus Christ. It's an Abrahamic and monotheistic religion, which means:

Abrahamic – The teachings of Christianity descend and originate from the ancient Israelites, such as Abraham. This means that Christians worship the God of Abraham (sometimes referred to as Yahweh).

Monotheistic – Christians only believe in one god. The term 'monotheistic' comes from the ancient Greek 'monos' ('single') and 'theos' ('god'). In contrast, some religions are polytheistic (belief in multiple gods), such as the ancient Egyptian and Roman faiths. An example of a modern polytheistic religion would be Shinto, a major religion in Japan.

So, Christians only believe in one god, and this is the God of Abraham.

The Bible

The primary text of Christianity is the Bible. This book contains all of the most important rules and teachings which Christianity is based on. The Bible is divided into two major books: the Old Testament, and the New Testament.

The Old Testament is a collection of writings from the ancient Israelites. The Old Testament contains some of the most well-known parts of the

CHRISTIANITY AND CATHOLICISM

Bible, such as:

1. The Creation Story (The Story of Adam and Eve).

2. Noah's Ark, where God spares Noah, his family, and two of each animal, whilst flooding the rest of the world.

3. The Binding of Isaac, where Abraham is tested as God asks him to sacrifice his only son.

4. The ten plagues against Egypt, in which Moses frees the Hebrews from slavery under the Egyptians.

5. The Ten Commandments, where Moses climbs Mount Sinai and receives the Ten Commandments from God.

There are many more stories within the Old Testament, such as David and Goliath, Cain and Abel, and the Tower of Babel. On top of this, the Old Testament contains poetry and rules.

The Old Testament is divided into the following books:

1. **Genesis** – This includes the Creation Story, the Flood, all the way up to the birth of Joseph.

2. **Exodus** – This mostly focuses on the story of Moses, through God, freeing the Hebrews from Egypt. This also contains the Ten Commandments.

3. **Leviticus** – This book primarily contains a list of rules and laws that the people of Israel should follow.

4. **Numbers** – This book follows the Israelites as they travel from Mount Sinai to Canaan.

5. **Deuteronomy** – This focuses on Moses guiding the Israelites to the Promised Land.

6. **Joshua, Judges, Samuel, and Kings** – These four books focus on the history of Israel as it starts to become a world power.

7. **Books of Maccabees** – These books contain the story of Jewish rebellion against an Ancient Greek family, the Seleucids.

8. **Isaiah, Jeremiah, Ezekiel, and Daniel** – These are the twelve major prophets of the Old Testament, who continue to build on the teachings established in the Old Testament.

9. **Job, Proverbs, Ecclesiastes, Psalms, Song of Solomon** – Sometimes referred to as the books of wisdom, these include more rules and guidelines, along with poetry which sheds more light on the nature of God.

The second major part of the Bible is the New Testament. This primarily follows the life of Jesus Christ from the perspective of multiple authors. The New Testament consists of the following books:

1. **The four canonical (accepted by the Church) gospels** – The Gospels of Matthew, Mark, Luke, and John. These four gospels were written by different authors and at different times. While they all focus on Jesus' life, they don't always cover the same points in his life. For example, Mark's Gospel begins at Jesus' baptism, approximately thirty years into his life.

2. **Acts of the Apostles** – This book follows the apostles as they continue Christ's work after his death and resurrection.

3. **Epistles** – This book encompasses holy letters, most of which were written by Paul to different churches, people, and other bodies.

4. **Book of Revelation** – This book is an account of the return of Jesus Christ and the apocalypse. This is the final book of the Bible.

While the Bible is one book that all Christians follow, different denominations will prefer different editions and translations. This means that, for example, there will be differences between the Catholic Bible and a Bible which a protestant might use.

Additionally, there have been multiple different translations of the Bible throughout history. While the content mostly remains the same between them, phrasing and terminology will differ. This can also impact the numbering of passages in the Bible that you're reading. For this reason, it's important to find out which Bible your GCSE course uses. In many cases, you can find online publications of the Bible, saving you from having to purchase a physical copy.

The Ten Commandments

Like most religions, Christianity is rule-based. By this, we mean that the religion is full of rules and guidelines which followers are expected to obey. Morals, rules and guidelines appear throughout the Bible in the form of sermons and stories, but none are as clear as the Ten

CHRISTIANITY AND CATHOLICISM

Commandments. These are the ten laws that all Christians must follow, and cover everything from killing and theft to honouring one's parents and lying.

The Ten Commandments first appear in the second book of the Old Testament: Exodus. However, they also appear in Deuteronomy. The Ten Commandments were given to Moses by God after the Hebrews escaped from Egypt. Moses climbed to the top of Mount Sinai, and returned with two tablets which had the Commandments inscribed into them.

The exact formulation and translation of the Ten Commandments differs depending on the Bible you read. However, they all contain the following rules:

COMMANDMENT 1

I am the Lord thy God, thou shalt have no other gods before me.

COMMANDMENT 2

Thou shalt not make unto thee any graven image.

COMMANDMENT 3

Thou shalt not take the name of the Lord thy God in vain.

COMMANDMENT 4

Remember the sabbath day, to keep it holy.

COMMANDMENT 5

Honour thy father and thy mother.

COMMANDMENT 6

Thou shalt not kill.

COMMANDMENT 7

Thou shalt not commit adultery.

COMMANDMENT 8

Thou shalt not steal.

COMMANDMENT 9

Thou shalt not bear false witness against thy neighbour.

COMMANDMENT 10

Thou shalt not covet.

Some of these are rather clear, such as "Thou shalt not kill." However, some of the commandments need further explanation. Here is what each commandment is generally interpreted to mean:

Commandment	Meaning
I am the Lord thy God, thou shalt have no other gods before me.	This states that God is the god of the Israelites, and also their *only* god. They may not worship any other gods.
Thou shalt not make unto thee any graven image.	This is a continuation of the first commandment, stating that we are not to create idols (or idolise) for things that are not God.
Thou shalt not take the name of the Lord thy God in vain.	This commandment states that we should not use the Lord's name in vain. God is telling us not to use his name in trivial circumstances, and to only use it during prayer and other forms of worship.
Remember the sabbath day, to keep it holy.	This outlines that the sabbath day is important and must be preserved for worship and rest.
Honour thy father and thy mother.	This commandment is quite straight-forward: respect and obey your parents, but can also extend to your ancestry as a whole.
Thou shalt not kill.	God commands us not to kill.
Thou shalt not commit adultery.	God states that we should not have a sexual relationship with anyone other than who we are married to.
Thou shalt not steal.	God commands us not to steal.
Thou shalt not bear false witness against thy neighbour.	This commandment tells us not to lie. However, some interpret this as a command to never lie while under oath, such as in a court of law.
Thou shalt not covet.	While most other commandments are focused on actions, this one focuses on thought. God commands us not to be envious of other peoples' belongings.

Here, we've tried to highlight the most common interpretation for each of the Ten Commandments. However, there is still a lot of debate over the true meaning of each commandment.

Additionally, some Christians believe that the Ten Commandments are ranked in order of importance. This means that the first commandment is the most important, and the tenth commandment is the least important. However, other Christians believe that the commandments are equally important.

All Christians believe that breaking one of these commandments is a sin, since you are acting directly against God's commands.

There are more rules in the Bible, most of which can be found in Leviticus. However, these aren't as universally followed by Christians – partially because there are lots of them!

Key Differences Between Christianity and Catholic Christianity (Catholicism)

As previously mentioned, the GCSE Religious Studies course expects you to have an understanding of both Christianity and Catholic Christianity. To make things simpler, we've decided to lay out the most important differences between the two faiths. For the sake of contrast, we will be pointing out the differences between Protestant Christianity and Catholic Christianity.

Scripture
Most Protestant Christians adopt the doctrine of "Sola Skriptura". This essentially means that the only book which Protestants must follow is the Bible.

In contrast, Catholics base their beliefs on multiple different scriptures and codes alongside the Bible. Catholics, for example, follow the doctrine of the Catholic Church, which is outlined and detailed in the Catechism.

Leadership
The leader of the Catholic Church is the Pope. The Pope is significant because they are believed to be a successor of Saint Peter, who Catholics believe to be the first Pope and the founder of the Church. Many Catholics believe that the Pope is God's messenger on Earth.

Besides being a figurehead, the Pope is expected to guide Catholic doctrine through the modern world.

In contrast, Protestants are not obliged to follow the doctrine laid out by the Pope. Instead, individual churches will have their own leadership. For example, the head of the Church of England is the Archbishop of Canterbury.

Consecration and Priesthood
In the Catholic Church, priesthood isn't just an important role which incurs responsibility. It's part of a succession of priests throughout history known as the 'apostolic succession'. In essence, priesthood is a role being passed down through history, from the origins of the Catholic Church all the way to the modern day. This means that, since priesthood is a sacrament, there are strict requirements for becoming a priest, and even stricter rules which priests must follow. For example, women are not permitted to become priests in the Catholic Church.

In most Protestant organisations, priesthood does not carry the same kind of holy weight. Nevertheless, it's still an incredibly prominent position to hold, and still incurs a number of responsibilities. In many Protestant Churches, women are allowed to become priests.

The Eucharist
The Eucharist, also known as the Lord's Supper, is the point at which Holy Communion takes place. You might be familiar with this sacrament: members of the congregation eat bread and wine to accept Jesus into their lives. There are a number of differences here for Catholics and Protestants.

In the Catholic Church, the bread and wine are consecrated by the priest. Catholics believe that, once this occurs, the bread and wine actually *become* the body and blood of Jesus. In other words, the bread and wine become embodiments of Jesus Christ. This is known as *Transubstantiation*.

In contrast, the Protestant Church does not accept the doctrine that the bread and wine literally transform into the body and blood of Christ. Instead, the Eucharist acts to commemorate Jesus' death and resurrection by re-enacting the Last Supper.

Sacraments

In the Catholic Church, there are seven sacraments. We will discuss these in more detail later in this chapter, so for now here are their names:

1. Baptism.
2. Confirmation.
3. The Eucharist.
4. Matrimony (Marriage).
5. Penance (Confession).
6. Holy Orders (e.g. Priesthood).
7. Anointing of the Sick (sometimes known as 'Last Rites').

In the Protestant Church, only two of these sacraments are formally practised: Baptism and The Eucharist.

On top of these major theological and structural differences, the Catholic and Protestant Churches have differing views on a number of moral, political, philosophical, and social issues. These will be discussed in more detail during Unit 2 of this book.

As you can see, there are many differences between the Catholic Church and the Protestant Church. Many of these have a significant impact on the way the churches practice their faiths, so it's important that you learn the major differences between them.

These are the major differences between Catholicism and Protestantism. For the following sections, we will be discussing more general core beliefs in Christianity. Any differences between the churches which appear during that discussion will be made clear.

The Core Beliefs of Christianity

Now that we have a foundational understanding of Christianity, the Bible, and the differences between Christianity and Catholic Christianity, we can move onto the core beliefs of Christianity. In particular, we'll be taking a look at the following key aspects of Christianity:

- The Holy Trinity;
- The Creation Story;

- Sin and Original Sin;
- Transubstantiation and Consubstantiation;
- Christmas and Easter.

The Holy Trinity

The Holy Trinity is the doctrine of Christianity which explains the connection between God, Jesus Christ, and the Holy Spirit (also known as the Holy Ghost). The Holy Trinity describes the relationship between the three. God the Father, Jesus Christ the Son, and the Holy Spirit are three separate entities. At the same time, they are all also God.

So that means that God is:

1. The Father.
2. The Son.
3. The Holy Spirit.

While these are all God, they are also separate. Additionally, this does not mean that the Father and the Holy Spirit are the same thing. Most Christian denominations call the Holy Trinity a mystery – recognising the fact that it is a puzzle which cannot be solved by human logic or reasoning.

The following image, The Shield of the Trinity, shows the connection between God, the Father, Jesus Christ the Son, and the Holy Spirit.

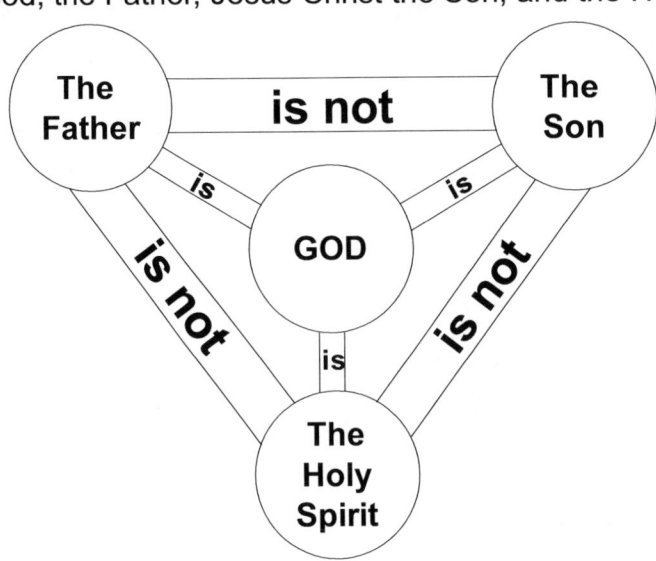

Now, let's take a look at the three entities of the Holy Trinity:

God the Father
When people talk about God as the creator and caretaker of the universe, they are usually referring to God the Father. The Father is the depiction of God that tends to appear in paintings and popular culture: a huge man with long hair and a beard. God the Father is the entity of the Holy Trinity which is principally responsible for the creation of the universe and everything within it.

God the Son
God the Son is Jesus Christ. Jesus is the son of God, but at the same time is also God, since he's a member of the Holy Trinity. We'll talk about Jesus in more detail later in this chapter, but here are a few things to know before moving forward:

1. Jesus is considered by Christians to be the son of God, the king who was spoken about in Old Testament prophecy.

2. Christians believe that Jesus died on the cross to absolve (or cleanse) us of our sins.

3. Jesus rose from the dead on Easter Sunday, proving that there is life after death.

The Holy Spirit
While God the Father and God the Son are depicted as singular, human-like entities, the Holy Spirit is a lot more abstract. By this, we mean that the Holy Spirit doesn't take a physical form in the Bible, and doesn't interact with the world in the same way that Jesus did. The best way to describe the Holy Spirit is that it is God's continued presence in the world, existing everywhere and working in the world to put God's will into practice. The Holy Spirit appears at numerous points during the New Testament after Jesus' death. The Holy Spirit is often depicted in paintings and other art as a dove, but the Bible does not give it a physical form.

The Creation Story

The creation story, also known as the story of Adam and Eve, is perhaps one of the most well-known and frequently discussed parts of the Bible. The creation story details the creation of all things by God. God creates the world over the course of six days at the beginning of Genesis, and rests on the seventh day. Here's how the creation story plays out.

Opening
Before God begins to create the world, it is described as being "formless and void."

The First Day
On the first day, God creates light, divides light from the darkness, and then creates day and night.

The Second Day
On the second day, God creates heaven. In fact, according to Genesis, he creates Heaven from the water on the currently shapeless Earth.

The Third Day
Now that there is light and dark, day and night, and Heaven, God proceeds to create land, as well as the plants and trees which inhabit land. God also names the bodies of water between the land as 'seas'.

The Fourth Day
On the fourth day, God creates two great lights, one to rule the day, and the other (the lesser) to rule the night. Presumably, these two great lights are the sun and the moon. Additionally, the stars are created on this day.

The Fifth Day
On the fifth day, God creates fish to inhabit the seas, as well as birds to fly above the earth. Additionally, God creates "the great sea-monsters." God commands these animals to "be fruitful and multiply" – to reproduce.

The Sixth Day
On the sixth day, God turns his attention to the "beasts of the earth." At this point, creatures such as cattle are created to inhabit the land. After this, God creates humans.

When making humans, God states "Let us make man in our image, after our likeness; and let them have dominion over the fish of the sea, and over the fowl of the air, and over the cattle, and over all the earth, and over every creeping thing that creepeth upon the earth." This demonstrates that God gave us, human beings, stewardship and dominance over the earth. God also commands humans to "be fruitful and multiply."

This is also the point in the Bible where it is clear that God made humans in his image and likeness. As previously mentioned, this does not necessarily mean that God looks like a human being. Rather, it means that humans share some of the qualities that God also possesses.

The Seventh Day

On the seventh day, God does not create anything. Instead, he rests on the seventh day, and also blesses it. This is where the tradition of the Sabbath comes from!

The Creation Story: Truth or Fiction?

The Old Testament presents the creation story as though it actually happened. Unlike Jesus' parables, which are clearly stories designed to deliver a message, the creation story is written as though the events are supposed to be taken literally. This has led many Christians to accept the creation story as fact. The belief that the creation story literally happened is called literalism or fundamentalism.

When taken literally, the creation story contradicts our current scientific understanding of the world. For example, God creates light and dark on the first day, but creates the sun and moon on the fourth day. As we know, the sun is what shines light on the earth and the rest of the solar system. This means that the details of the story in Genesis are inaccurate.

Additionally, the creation story neglects to mention other phenomena that we have discovered, such as dinosaurs or evolution. From our current scientific understanding, humans weren't just made, and aren't necessarily distinct from other animals. Rather, evolutionary theory states that humans evolved from other creatures. The creation story does not mention this at all.

While some choose to interpret the creation story literally, others treat it more like a parable. Rather than sweating the details, these Christians take away a few key points from the story:

1. God created the world and everything in it. How he did so isn't the point.
2. God created humans in his image and likeness.
3. God gave humans dominion over the world.
4. God commanded humans to reproduce.

5. God rested on the seventh day and blessed it, giving us the sabbath.

Sin and Original Sin
A central aspect of Christianity, as well as other world religions, is sin. To commit a sin is to commit an act which is considered immoral in the eyes of God. If you commit a sin, you are damaging the relationship between yourself and God. For example, one of the Ten Commandments is "thou shalt not kill." Therefore, if you killed someone, you would be committing a sin. Most Christians believe that, if you live in sin, you risk being sent to Hell for eternity.

However, committing a sin doesn't necessarily mean you are condemned forever. Most Christian denominations teach that, because God is benevolent (all-loving), he is willing to forgive even our worst sins if we repent. The process of admitting and apologising for our sins is usually referred to as "absolution." During this process, we confess the sins which we have committed. If God deems us to be truly sorry, he absolves us of our sins.

Original Sin
After God created humans in the form of Adam and Eve, the two were allowed to exist in the paradise of Eden. However, the pair were tempted by a snake, an embodiment of evil, to eat fruit from a tree which God had forbade them from eating. The only command that God gave to Adam and Eve was to not eat from that tree, so when God discovered that they had, he cast them out of Eden. This is known as the 'original sin', and the root of all sin in the world today.

This original sin is used by the Bible to explain the existence of evil and suffering in the world, as Adam and Eve live relatively horrible lives after they are cast out of Eden. Thousands of years later, Jesus Christ would die to forgive us for the original sin.

When Christians are baptised, they are being cleansed of original sin. This is one of the reasons why baptism is such an important part of many Christian denominations.

Christmas and Easter
Two of the most important dates in the Christian calendar are Christmas and Easter. Christmas celebrates Jesus' birth in Bethlehem, while Easter commemorates how Jesus rose from the dead on Easter Sunday. Let's take a look at both of these holidays in more detail.

Christmas

Christmas is an important date in the Christian calendar because it celebrates the birth of Jesus. Here's a breakdown of the Christmas story (also known as the Nativity):

1. Mary, Jesus' mother, is visited by the archangel Gabriel, and is told that she will bear a child. She is told to name the child Jesus, or Emmanuel ('God with us').

2. The Roman Empire, who controlled the territory in which Mary and Joseph lived, hold a census. Everyone is expected to return to their hometown for the census to be carried out. Since Joseph was from Bethlehem, the couple must depart for Bethlehem.

3. When they arrive in Bethlehem, they find that all of the inns are full. The only place they can find is a stable, in which Jesus is born.

4. Jesus is visited by the Three Kings and local shepherds.

5. After some time, Mary, Joseph, and Jesus return to Nazareth via Egypt, since they are warned that King Herod wishes to kill Jesus.

There are some important details to know about the Nativity:

1. Mary is impregnated by God, and is therefore still a virgin when she gives birth to Jesus.

2. Even though Jesus is the son of God and the king foretold in prophecy, he is not born into a noble household. Joseph, his human father, is a carpenter.

3. Jesus is born in a stable, rather than a palace or even an inn. This demonstrates that, despite being the son of God, Jesus is born into humble circumstances.

Advent is the period of time building up to the birth of Jesus Christ, from the time when Mary and Joseph left Nazareth to depart for Bethlehem. Gifts are given as part of the Christmas tradition today in order to represent the gifts given to Jesus by the Three Kings.

Easter

For many Christians, Easter is the most important holiday in the Christian calendar. This is because it is steeped in meaning and morals. Christians believe that we can learn a lot about Jesus, and God, from the days leading up to Jesus' death and resurrection. Here's a summary of the Easter story, from Ash Wednesday all the way up to Easter Sunday.

1. Ash Wednesday marks the first day of Lent, the period during which Jesus spent forty days and forty nights in the wilderness, avoiding temptation from the Devil. The forty days parallels the forty years that the Israelites spent wandering the desert in the Old Testament.

2. After forty days passed, Jesus returned to civilisation. Approximately three years pass, during which Jesus performs miracles and teaches the gospel to those who will listen.

3. The Sunday before Easter Sunday is known as Palm Sunday. On this day, Christians believe that Jesus rode into Jerusalem on a donkey. This is significant because the Old Testament prophecy stated that the King of the Jews would ride into Jerusalem. Here, Jesus was clearly proclaiming to be this king. As Jesus entered Jerusalem, followers and on-lookers placed palm leaves in the road to make a path for Jesus. This is why the day is named 'Palm Sunday'.

4. The next significant day in Holy Week is Maundy Thursday. On this day, Jesus attended the Last Supper with his disciples, broke bread and drank wine.

5. The day after Maundy Thursday is Good Friday. After the Last Supper, Jesus went to the Garden of Gethsemane, where he prayed to God and admitted that he was afraid of what was to come. After this, Jesus is captured by the Romans. Judas, one of Jesus' disciples, had accepted thirty pieces of silver to betray Jesus. It is on this day that Jesus is crucified. After Jesus' death on the cross, he is buried in a tomb.

6. The next significant day is Easter Sunday. Jesus' tomb is found to be empty. Jesus is resurrected and meets with his disciples once again.

7. Jesus spent the next forty days on earth before being carried to Heaven.

Easter is an incredibly important time for Christians for a number of reasons:

1. On Palm Sunday, Jesus rode into Jerusalem on a donkey rather

than a horse. This is important because it shows that Jesus was humble.

2. Jesus spent forty days and forty nights in the desert, far from any luxuries. During this time, Satan tried to tempt him, but Jesus abstained. This is why many Christians give up something during Lent.

3. The Eucharist, which we mentioned earlier in this chapter, is based on the Last Supper. Christians eat bread and drink wine to remember the Last Supper and Jesus' sacrifice.

4. After Jesus' capture at the hands of the Romans, many of his disciples either pretended not to know him, or fled in a state of panic. However, Jesus forgave his disciples for this. This shows how Jesus, and therefore God, is forgiving.

5. Jesus was captured by the Romans because religious leaders in Jerusalem found him to be blasphemous. He claimed to be the son of God, but the religious institutions in Jerusalem did not believe this to be true.

6. Crucifixion is believed to be an extremely painful way to die, and it is not dignified either. Jesus probably died an agonising death, and Christians believe that this is so that our sins could be forgiven. In other words, Jesus died on the cross to absolve humanity for all of its sins.

7. Crucifixion was not a death reserved for nobles. Jesus died alongside common thieves and other criminals. This reflected how Jesus spent a lot of his ministry living with society's outcasts, forgiving wrongdoers who were truly sorry for their sins.

8. Jesus' resurrection on Easter Sunday demonstrates that there is life after death, and also that Jesus is the son of God.

The Life of Jesus Christ

Considering that Jesus is the central character in Christianity, his life is not easily summarised! However, you might have to answer questions about Jesus' life. So, we've summarised the key points that you need to know about the life of Jesus Christ.

1. Jesus was born to Mary, who was a virgin, in the town of Bethlehem. Sometime after his birth, Mary, Joseph, and Jesus returned to

Nazareth.

2. Since Joseph was a carpenter by profession, Jesus learnt carpentry. It is believed that he worked as a carpenter between the ages of twelve and thirty.

3. Jesus' ministry (teaching) began when he was approximately thirty years old. After being baptised in the River Jordan by John the Baptist, Jesus spent time in the wilderness, avoiding temptation from the Devil.

4. After returning from the wilderness, Jesus spent time gathering followers and preaching the gospel. During this period, he met his 12 disciples (known as the Apostles): Peter (also known as Simon Peter), Andrew, James (son of Zebedee), John, Philip, Bartholomew, Thomas, Matthew, James (son of Alphaeus), Judas Thaddeus, Simon the Canaanite, and Judas Iscariot.

5. During this time, Jesus performed miracles. For example, he turned water into wine at a wedding, demonstrating that God wants people to be happy. In addition, he raised Lazarus from the dead, fed five-thousand people with only a few loaves of bread and some fish, and healed the sick.

6. Jesus also used methods of storytelling in order to convey a message about the gospel (God's word). These are known as parables. One such parable was about the Good Samaritan: a man who helped a foreigner who was in need, despite a bitter relationship between their two nations. The message of this story was that God wants us to love, help, and forgive people – even our enemies.

7. Jesus also gave sermons and preached God's word on numerous noteworthy occasions. One such event was the Sermon on the Mount, in which Jesus presented the Beatitudes.

8. Jesus' final week before his death is known as Holy Week, which you can read about in our sub-section on Christmas and Easter on page 31.

9. After his resurrection, Jesus spent forty days on earth alongside his disciples before ascending to Heaven.

Here are a few more details about Jesus' personality and teachings:

1. Jesus' central tenet (teaching) is one of loving others, including

CHRISTIANITY AND CATHOLICISM

your enemies. This includes forgiving those who have wronged you.

2. Jesus regularly preached about non-violence and pacifism. However, he did express violence. He drove the tradesmen out of the temple in Jerusalem, overturning tables to scare them away.

3. Jesus also regularly taught about charity. Jesus once said "It is easier for a camel to go through the eye of a needle, than for a rich man to enter into the kingdom of God." (Mark 10:25, King James Bible). Jesus spent his ministry in what we would probably describe as poverty, and had minimal possessions. He encouraged his disciples to do the same.

4. While Jesus had twelve Apostles, others followed him as well. One such individual was Mary Magdalene, a prostitute. Jesus spent a lot of his ministry living alongside prostitutes, criminals, and others who were generally disliked by society.

5. Jesus was aware of his fate, and on a few occasions showed fear or agony. In the Garden of Gethsemane, shortly before his death, Jesus prayed to God, stating that "the spirit is willing, but the flesh is weak." This means that Jesus wanted to fulfil his purpose and die on the cross for humanity's sins, but his human nature made him afraid of it. This reminds us that Jesus, despite being the son of God and part of the Holy Trinity, was human.

Life, Death, and the Afterlife

One of the biggest parts of almost any religion is its approach to and teachings on life, death, and the afterlife. Christianity, like many modern religions, has the following core beliefs when it comes to the life, death, and the afterlife:

1. Human life is a gift from God. Therefore, all human life is sacred.

2. In addition, humans are believed to have been created in God's image and likeness. This makes humans distinct, and arguably more important, than all other animals.

3. Since all human life is considered sacred in Christianity, this means that most Christians are committed to the preservation of human life. This means that most committed Christians are morally opposed to abortion, euthanasia, and conflict. This will be discussed in more

detail in Chapter 7.

4. Christians believe that, since humans are created in God's image, they possess a soul. While the body is mortal and eventually dies, the soul is considered to be immortal.

5. Christians believe that they will be judged by God after they die, and this will determine whether they go to Heaven or Hell for eternity.

6. Heaven is a paradise in which our souls are reunited with God for eternity, whilst Hell is the exact opposite.

7. The Catholic Church teaches the doctrine of Purgatory. This is a place in which people who have sinned during life are purged of their sins before entering heaven. Most Christian denominations do not accept purgatory.

Human Life is a Gift from God, and Humans were Created in His Image and Likeness

As the creation story tells us, God created human beings as an act of love. Whether interpreted literally or as a metaphorical parable (a story with a moral message or specific meaning), the creation story makes it clear that human beings are created in God's image and likeness:

> "So God created humankind in his image, in the image of God he created them; male and female he created them." (New Revised Standard Version, Genesis 1:27)

Note: when Christians say that humans are created in God's image and likeness, this does not necessarily mean that God looks like a human being! Rather, 'image and likeness' refers to how our souls are similar to God's, potentially in the following ways:

1. Human beings have a soul.

2. Human beings have free will.

3. Human beings have dominion over the world.

The Immortality of the Soul

Christians believe that, although the body eventually dies, the soul lives on forever. This means that it is immortal. This is stated at a number of points in the Bible, such as the following from Ecclesiastes:

> "Then shall the dust return to the earth as it was: and the spirit shall return unto God who gave it." (King James Bible, Ecclesiastes 12:7)

If the soul is immortal, then there must be a place for it to go once the body dies. Christians believe that these two places are Heaven and Hell.

Judgement, Heaven, and Hell
The Bible reiterates that, after death, all human beings will be judged on their actions during their lives. If God deems someone to have lived a good Christian life, then that person's soul will enter Heaven. If they have not, then they will be sent to Hell.

The difference between Heaven and Hell is clear. Heaven is a place where good souls reunite with God for eternity. In contrast, Hell is a place absent of God's presence. As time has progressed, the depictions of Heaven and Hell have become more graphic, with works such as Dante's *Divine Comedy* portraying Hell as a place of fire, brimstone, and demons, whilst Heaven is inhabited by angels and other celestial beings.

While these are common depictions of Heaven and Hell in popular culture, Christians are not required to believe in any of these specific details. All Christians are expected to believe is that Heaven is a place where souls are reunited with God, and Hell is a place devoid of God's presence.

There is, however, one other place where human souls might go to after their bodies die. The Catholic Church teaches the doctrine of Purgatory: a kind of 'temporary hell' that some sinners might be sent to if they have sinned in life but can still be redeemed. This means that people have a second chance of arriving in Heaven after they die, provided that they serve their time in Purgatory. However, the majority of other Christian denominations do not believe in Purgatory, primarily because it is not explicitly referred to in the Bible.

The Sacraments, Prayer, and Worship
While incredibly important, reading the Bible and attending church are only part of the wider Christian faith for many denominations. Here, we'll take a look at the ways in which different people practise their faith.

The Sacraments

Sacraments are Christian rituals which are performed as part of the Christian faith. As discussed in our section on the differences between Catholics and other Christians, different denominations practice different numbers of sacraments. For example, the Catholic Church recognises seven sacraments, whilst other Protestant Churches only practice two or three. Let's take a look at all seven of the sacraments practised by the Catholic Church. Where applicable, practices for other denominations will be discussed.

The Sacraments of Initiation

The first three sacraments undertaken by Catholics are known as the sacraments of initiation. This is because they initiate a Catholic into the faith. These three sacraments are Baptism, Confirmation, and the Eucharist.

Baptism

Baptism is the first sacrament undertaken by a Christian. Baptism often takes place when the participant is quite young, such as when they are a baby or toddler. In this case, the parents or guardians of the child are making the decision to introduce and initiate them into the church. A small amount of holy water is usually poured onto the head of the child, while the member of the clergy (such as a Priest) states "I baptise you in the name of the Father and of the Son, and of the Holy Spirit."

However, people can choose to be baptised at an older age, if they were never baptised as a child. Sometimes, these baptisms occur with a larger body of water. In some churches, such as Evangelical and Baptist Churches, the priest or preacher will completely submerge the individual in water while they are being baptised.

A central concept in baptism is the cleansing of sins, including the Original Sin of Adam and Eve. This is why many choose to have their children baptised at a young age. The practice resembles Jesus' own baptism at the hands of John the Baptist in the New Testament. Baptism is a sacrament adopted in all Christian denominations.

People are usually only baptised once in their life, but in some traditions, baptisms are more regular. In some cases, individuals might request to be baptised again later in their life if they've rediscovered their faith.

The Eucharist (Holy Communion)

The Eucharist is the sacrament of accepting Jesus into one's own body and soul by eating bread and drinking wine. This commemorates the events of the Last Supper, at which Jesus and his disciples celebrated Passover. In many churches, the bread symbolises Jesus' body, whilst the wine symbolises his blood. When partaking in the Eucharist, Christians are remembering that Jesus sacrificed his own life to cleanse them of their sins.

In the Catholic Church, the Eucharist has even greater significance. Catholics believe that the bread and wine actually transforms into the body and blood of Jesus once consecrated by a Priest.

Christians will generally partake in the Eucharist multiple times in their life. Church services will often have a segment devoted to the Eucharist, so some Christians might be partaking in the Eucharist once per week.

Confirmation

Confirmation is a sacrament which focuses on individuals *confirming* their faith and their involvement in the Church. Usually, this occurs when the individual is in their mid or late teenage years, when they are in a position to make their own mind up about their faith. This is often considered to be a rite of passage into adulthood in the Catholic Church. Generally speaking, individuals only partake in Confirmation once in their life.

The Sacraments of Healing

There are two sacraments of healing practised by the Catholic Church. These sacraments focus on spiritual healing.

Confession

Confession, also known as penance or reconciliation, occurs when a Christian attends a session where they confess their sins (usually to a Priest). Sometimes, these occur in confession booths to help maintain anonymity. The purpose of Confession is for the individual to confess their sins, and to be forgiven by God. Confession proceeds as follows:

1. **Contrition** – the individual, or penitent, express genuine remorse for their wrongdoings. If they are not genuinely remorseful, Christians believe that they will not be forgiven.

2. **Confession** – the penitent attends Confession, where they

confess their sins to a priest. In the Catholic Church, only a priest is empowered to give the sacrament of Confession.

3. **Absolution** – this is when the priest absolves (forgives) the penitent of their sins. Christians believe that God forgives the penitent through the priest.

4. **Penance** – this is when the priest recommends a course of action for the penitent to take to complete Confession. Sometimes, they may be asked to pray or donate money or time to a charity. In more serious cases, such as when the penitent has committed a crime, the priest may recommend that they turn themselves in.

An important thing to remember about confession is that priests take an oath called the "Seal of Confessional". This means that they cannot speak about anything mentioned at the confession ever again. For example, if a penitent confesses to a crime during confession, the priest cannot inform the police. This is also known as priest-penitent privilege.

Practising Catholics usually attend confession multiple times in their life. Some Catholics will attend confession regularly, whilst others might only attend when they believe they have committed a sin. Confession is strictly a Catholic sacrament, although other denominations might provide an informal kind of confession.

Anointing of the Sick

This sacrament, sometimes known as 'last rites', is administered to Catholics who are either terminally ill or have reached an old age, close to death. This sacrament is administered by a priest, with the priest marking the patient's forehead with olive oil or plant oil, which reciting prayers. The purpose of this sacrament is to do the following:

1. Unite the sick person with Christ.

2. Give the patient and their family strength in the patient's final days.

3. Forgive the sins of the patient.

4. Hope for the restoration of the patient's health, even if it seems unlikely or even impossible.

5. Prepare the patient for passing into the afterlife.

This sacrament is sometimes offered to people before undertaking major surgery. In the unfortunate event that the patient dies during the operation, they will have taken their last rites.

The Sacraments of Service
These sacraments are concerned with service to the Church, oneself, and to God.

Holy Orders
This sacrament is undertaken by bishops, priests, and deacons in the Catholic Church. These individuals are expected to become an image of Christ, and must take on certain vows. All priests take a vow of chastity (to never have sex or marry). Some priests, but not all, take a vow of poverty. This means that they must limit their personal belongings.

Matrimony (Marriage)
Matrimony is the sacrament of marriage. Christians believe that marriage ceremonies, especially when taking place in a church, are in the presence of God. The two participants in the marriage take vows to each other and to the church, and enter a covenant (contract) with each other and God. Rings are usually exchanged as a symbol of this covenant.

ISLAM

Now that you've had a chance to learn about Christianity, it's time to take a look at another major world religion: Islam.

In this chapter, we'll be taking a look at the following areas:

1. What is Islam?
2. The Qur'an.
3. The Key Differences Between Sunni and Shi'a Muslims.
4. Core Principles of Islam.
5. The Nature of Allah.
6. The Life of the Prophet Muhammed.
7. Life, Death, and the Afterlife.
8. Muslim Worship and Festivals.

What is Islam?

Like Christianity and Judaism, Islam is one of the three major Abrahamic religions. As previously discussed in our chapter on Christianity, this means that writing on God in Islam (Allah), comes from the same god which Abraham interacted with in the Old Testament. Similar to Christianity and Judaism, Islam is monotheistic: there is only one god in Islam.

Of the three major religions we're discussing in this book, Islam is the youngest. The religion was formed in the 7th Century, while Christianity is approximately 2,000 years old, and Judaism is around 3,500 years old.

The main holy text for Muslims is the Qur'an. While this contains stories and themes which are similar to the Bible and the Torah, particularly in the Old Testament, the Qur'an is different in a number of ways. On top of the Qur'an, the Prophet Muhammed's teachings are read, studied, and followed by Muslims. Some of these teachings appear in places other than the Qur'an.

Aside from Allah Himself, Muhammed is the most important figure in Islam. Muslims believe him to be the final in a long line of prophets, and therefore his teachings are of utmost importance. Muslims also believe that Allah chose Muhammed to be His messenger on Earth, and revealed the Qur'an to him. During his life, Muhammed was the founder and leader of the Muslim faith.

Despite being relatively young, Islam is one of the biggest religions in the entire world. Approximately 25% of the world's population (1.8 billion people) are Muslim, making it the fastest-growing major religion in the world. The three holiest sites in Islam are Mecca, Medina, and Jerusalem. The name of the place of worship which Muslims attend is called a mosque.

The Qur'an

The Qur'an is the primary text of the Muslim faith. Unlike many Christians, who believe that the Bible is a human interpretation of God's word, Muslims tend to believe that the Qur'an is the most complete and accurate account of Allah's word. In fact, most Muslims believe that the Qur'an is Allah's exact words to Muhammed. For this reason, Muslims believe that the Qur'an is the ultimate source of knowledge about what is right and wrong, as well as the nature of Allah.

The Qur'an was originally written in Arabic. Many Muslims believe that, if it was translated to another language, the Qur'an would lose some of its meaning. For this reason, most Muslims learn Arabic so that they can appreciate the Qur'an in its original form.

Like many religious texts, the Qur'an is divided into chapters and verses. Chapters are known as 'surahs', and there are 114 of them. Each surah is made up of verses, which are known as 'ayahs'. Unlike other religious texts, the surahs in the Qur'an are ordered by their length. This means that the longest surahs appear at the start of the book, whilst the shortest ones appear towards the end. Muslims read the Qur'an both in private and public acts of worship.

Muslims attempt to keep their Qur'an in pristine condition. Many Muslims will wrap their Qur'an in cloth to prevent it from becoming dusty, and often clean their hands before using it. Muslims believe that the Qur'an itself is a miracle, and therefore treat it with the utmost care and respect.

Other Holy Texts

Aside from the Qur'an, there are other holy texts which are part of the Muslim faith. These include:

1. **Hadith** – Texts which account the life and deeds of Muhammed. These are not believed to be the word of Allah, but rather are reports from Muhammed's followers about his life. The Hadith are used to find out how Muhammed lived, and how Muslims can follow his example.

2. **Injil (Gospel of Jesus)** – A book given to Isa (Jesus) by Allah. Some Muslims believe that this book is similar to the Christian New Testament.

3. **Suhuf Ibrahim (Scrolls of Abraham)** – This book was believed to be given to Ibrahim (known as Abraham in the Christian faith) by Allah. This book is believed to have been lost to the passage of time, and is now only mentioned in other books such as the Qur'an.

4. **Sunnah** – The Sunnah outlines how Muhammed lived, giving Muslims further instruction on how to live a good Muslim life.

5. **Tawrat (Torah)** – This is the book given to Musa (Moses). While this is the primary Jewish holy text, many Muslims still believe it to be important.

6. **Zabur (Psalms)** – This is a book given to Dawud (David). Some Muslims believe that this book is connected to the Psalms of David in Christian and Jewish holy texts.

Note: All of these books are believed to have changed over time, unlike the Qur'an – which is still in its original form. Therefore, Muslims do not believe that these books are Allah's exact word.

The Key Differences Between Sunni and Shi'a Muslims

The Muslim population is divided into two denominations. These are known as 'Sunni' and 'Shi'a'.

The vast majority (approximately 90%) of Muslims are Sunni Muslims. These two groups formed after Ali, one of the first four caliphs (leaders), died. The Sunni Muslims accepted the next caliph after Ali, whilst the Shi'a followed his heritage and family.

Sunni and Shi'a Muslims share a lot of beliefs about Allah, the Qur'an, and the Prophet Muhammed. However, they have some key differences, such as:

Sunni Beliefs

Sunni Muslims believe that the direction that the faith takes should be decided on by Muslim communities. In other words, there is no single central leader, and decisions are to be made democratically.

Sunni Muslims believe that Muhammed was the last person to receive knowledge directly from Allah. Therefore, they do not place any emphasis on figures after Allah.

Shi'a Beliefs

Shi'a Muslims believe that Ali was an extremely important figure, whom Allah gave knowledge to in a similar way to Muhammed. Therefore, Shi'a Muslims follow the teachings of Ali and the imams, figureheads in the faith. Shi'a Muslims believe that imams are descendants of Muhammed.

Shi'a Islam has further internal splits, primarily due to the debate between how many true imams there are. Twelvers believe that there is a line of twelve imams, whilst Seveners place special emphasis on the seventh imam.

In addition, Sunni and Shi'a have different articles of faith. These are:

Sunni Articles of Faith

1. **Tawhid** – belief that Allah is the one and only god.
2. **Mala'ikah** – belief in the existence of angels (more on those later).
3. Belief in the holy books of Islam (e.g. the Qur'an).
4. **Nubuwwah** – belief in Allah's prophets, with the final prophet being Muhammed.
5. Belief in the day of judgement, in which all human souls will be judged by Allah.
6. **Predestination (al-Qadr)** – belief that Allah knows everything that will happen, and has already set out everything which will happen.

Shi'a Articles of Faith

1. **Tawhid** – belief that Allah is the one and only god.
2. **Adalat** – belief in divine justice (i.e. Allah exacted justice in the world).

3. **Nubuwwah** – belief in Allah's prophets.
4. **Imamah** – belief in the imams, and revering their authority.
5. **Ma'ad** – belief in the day of resurrection.

Core Principles of Islam

Islam is a faith built on a number of central principles. Let's take a look at some of those now.

Tawhid

Tawhid is the Islamic doctrine that there is only one god: Allah. The term 'Allah' roughly translates to 'the god', which drives home the message that there is only one god in Islam. This is similar to the first of the Jewish and Christian Ten Commandments: "I am the one true God; Thou shalt have no other gods but me".

Not only do Muslims believe that there is only one god, but also that faith in other gods, or idolatry (worship) of anything else but Allah is the absolute worst sin one can commit. This is called shirk. This does not apply just to other gods, but also to other aspects of the world. For example, if one idolised money more than Allah, this would be an example of shirk.

Shirk is also the reason why Muslims are not permitted to create imagery of Muhammed: creating images of Muhammed would draw attention from Allah.

Tawhid is part of the Shahadah, the Muslim declaration of faith.

The Five Pillars of Sunni Islam

The Five Pillars refer to the five obligations that Muslims have to fulfil in order to become closer to Allah and to live a good life. For Sunni Muslims, these are:

1. **Shahadah** – Reciting the declaration of faith.
2. **Salah** – Praying five times a day at set times. Muslims do this to keep Allah and the Muslim faith as a central part of their daily lives.
3. **Zakat** – Giving money to help the poor. Muslims are expected to give approximately one fortieth of their income to help the poor once per year. This is an important part of the Muslim faith as it

prevents greed.

4. **Sawm** – Fasting during Ramadan. Muslims who are in good health and have reached a mature age are expected to fast during the month of Ramadan to connect with Allah. It also serves as a reminder for many Muslims that they are fortunate to have food, while many in the world do not.

5. **Hajj** – Pilgrimage to Mecca. The pilgrimage occurs annually, in the twelfth month of the Muslim calendar. Many Muslims make this pilgrimage at least once in their life, so long as they can afford to and are in good health.

Angels and Prophets

Prophets and angels are present in Christianity and Judaism, but are much more central to the Muslim faith. Let's take a look at how angels and prophets impact the Muslim faith:

Angels

Angels ('mala'ikah') are celestial beings created by Allah to enact his will. Muslims believe that angels were created before humans, and primarily exist in an angelic realm. Angels are believed to not have free will, and exist to carry out Allah's commands.

In the Muslim faith, angels are described both as human-like (anthropomorphic) and also as abstract beings. In some cases, they appear as human-like creatures with wings, whilst in other cases appear as winged beings of pure light. Most Muslims believe that angels do not have genders, although many of their names are traditionally masculine.

There are different kinds of angels in the Muslim faith, and different angels fulfil different roles. For example, guardian angels are those which protect people and the world from evil. Other angels fulfil roles such as recording the deeds of people, both good and bad.

Angels also have a hierarchy (order of leadership), with archangels being of a higher ranking than other angels. All angels answer to Allah. Angels do not have free will, which means that they cannot sin.

Here are some of the most prominent angels in Islam – many of which have a parallel in Judaism and Christianity.

1. **Israfil (Raphael in the Judeo-Christian faiths)** – Muslims believe

that Israfil's presence will signify the day of judgement. It is believed that Israfil will usher in the day of judgement by sounding a trumpet.

2. **Izrail (Azrael)** – Izrail is the angel of death. While this might sound sinister, Izrail's role is to collect the souls of the dead and escort them to the afterlife.

3. **Jibril (Gabriel)** – Jibril's task is to deliver messages (or revelations) to important prophets, such as Muhammed. Muslims believe that Allah revealed His word through Jibril.

4. **Mika'il (Michael)** – Mika'il's role is to go to Allah and ask him to forgive people's sins.

Prophets

Prophets are also an important part of Islam. We'll discuss the most often discussed prophet in Islam, Muhammed, in a later section. For now, let's take a general look at the role of prophets in Islam.

Muslims believe that prophets were human beings who received messages from Allah. In other words, prophets experienced revelations about how to live a good life. Muslims believe that Allah did this so that he could keep humans on the right track, and try to prevent them from falling into sin. Human beings have free will, so they can choose to go against Allah's will if they wish. However, the prophets existed in order to give people all of the information that they needed to live a good life. In Islam, prophets are sometimes referred to as rasuls (messengers). It is believed that Allah revealed His message to the prophets using angels, such as Jibril.

While a lot of emphasis is placed on Muhammed, the final prophet, the Qur'an teaches that all prophets should be treated equally. Twenty-five prophets are mentioned in the Qur'an, such as Adam, Ibrahim, Isma'il, Isa, Musa, Dawud, and Muhammed. Some of these prophets performed miracles to demonstrate that they were not false prophets.

Jihad

Jihad means 'struggle', and is a part of the Muslim faith which recognises both internal struggle to follow Allah's teaching, as well as the external struggle to help improve the world. Generally speaking, there are two kinds of jihad in Islamic teachings: greater, and lesser.

Greater jihad focuses on one's internal struggle to follow Allah and the

Qur'an. This is an ongoing struggle for many Muslims as they attempt to follow Allah's teachings and instructions. Most Muslims believe that in order to serve the world (lesser jihad), one must be attempting to resolve their internal struggle.

Lesser jihad is concerned with trying to improve the world. This involves maintaining peace, trying to end poverty, and also to fight injustice. Muslims are also allowed to defend Islam as part of the lesser jihad, which has led some extremists to justify terrorism.

The Nature of Allah

An incredibly important part of any religion, including Islam, is the nature of its god. Muslims believe that Allah holds the following qualities:

1. **Benevolent** – Allah is believed to be all-loving and all-good (benevolent). Allah is incapable of committing sins or evil. He intervenes in the world because He loves and cares for His creation.

2. **Merciful** – Allah is perceived as being merciful. Almost every chapter of the Qur'an begins by reiterating this sentiment. Allah is willing to forgive people's sins.

3. **Omnipotent** – Muslims believe that Allah is all-powerful (omnipotent). Allah created the universe and everything within it, and has the power to perform miracles. Additionally, Allah is omniscient: He knows everything that has ever happened and will ever happen.

4. **Just** – Allah is believed to be just: He will judge each and every person fairly on the day of judgement.

5. **Transcendent** – Allah is the ultimate being, beyond everything else.

6. **Immanent** – Allah is involved in His creation (i.e. the universe). He intervenes in the world, and knows each and every person.

The Life of the Prophet Muhammed

Muslims believe that Muhammed is the final prophet in Islam, the founder of Islam, and the one whom Allah revealed the Qur'an to. He was born in the year 570 in Mecca, and died in the year 632. He was orphaned at a young age, and raised by his uncle.

Muslims believe that Muhammed was meditating, around the age of forty, when he was visited by Jibril: the angel of revelation. It was at this point in Muhammed's life that Allah's word was revealed to him. Over time, more and more was revealed to Muhammed by Jibril. Muhammed wrote what was revealed to him, resulting in the Qur'an.

The majority of Muslims believe that Muhammed was the final prophet – there will be no other prophets after him. For this reason, he is called the 'seal of the prophets'. He's considered to be an extremely important figure in Islam, and many people read the Hadith and Sunnah to find out how he lived and try to follow his example in their own lives.

As previously mentioned, Muslims are generally not permitted to create imagery of Muhammed, despite his significance in the faith. This is to prevent idolatry of Muhammed, since Muslims should be worshipping Allah directly instead. Despite this, Muhammed is highly respected by Muslims.

Life, Death, and the Afterlife

Just like Christianity and Judaism, Islam has a number of teachings about life, death, and the afterlife.

Al-Akhirah (The Afterlife)

Muslims believe that, after the Day of Judgement, all souls will pass on to the afterlife. Belief in the afterlife is a central part of Islam. Those who have lived good lives will enter Jannah ('Paradise'), whilst those who have lived in sin will be sent to Jahannam ('Hell'). Unlike Christianity, in which sinners can be sent to Hell for eternity, Islam teaches that even sinners in Jahannam can eventually go to Jannah. Muslims believe that this is because Allah is merciful and compassionate.

Yawm ad-Din (The Day of Judgement)

The Day of Judgement is the day on which Allah will decide who enters Jannah, and who is sent to Jahannam. Everyone will be judged based on their deeds in life, and the dead will be resurrected to be judged alongside the living. Actions and intentions are important, and Muslims believe that we will be judged on both.

Muslim Worship and Festivals

Worship takes many forms in Islam. In this section, we're going to be taking a look at the ways in which Muslims express and practice their faith.

Muslim Prayer

Salah is the Pillar of Islam which focuses on prayer. Muslims are expected to pray five times daily. If possible, these prayers should take place in a mosque. However, prayer can be practised anywhere. Muslims wash themselves before prayer – this practice is called wudu.

The times of day at which Muslims must pray are as follows: at dawn, just after midday, in the afternoon, at sunset, and in the evening/early night-time. Muslims recite verses from the Qur'an, which is why many Muslims try to learn the Qur'an by heart.

Muslim prayer involves the following actions:

1. **Stand to face Mecca** – Since this is the holiest site in Islam, Muslims must face Mecca when they pray. Muslims tend to learn whichever direction that they need to pray in, sometimes using a compass to direct them. This is called qiblah.

2. Raise hands to one's ears.

3. Fold one's arms cross their chest.

4. Bend over with hands on knees.

5. Stand, then prostrate on the floor.

6. Sit back on one's heels.

7. Turn the head left and right to demonstrate awareness of the angels.

Sunni Muslims tend to pray five times per day, but sometimes combine their prayers if they are travelling or otherwise will not be able to pray five times. Shi'a Muslims combine prayers more often, and might only pray three times per day.

Men are expected to attend a prayer session on Friday, known as Jummah, at a mosque. These prayers are led by an imam (prayer leader).

Muslims pray for a number of reasons. The first is to maintain reverence and respect for Allah ('taqwa'). It also helps Muslims to maintain discipline, and is also used to strengthen Muslim communities, as they all pray at the same time.

Traditionally, men and women would pray separately from each other. However, some mosques nowadays will allow for men and women to pray together in the same room. Often, women practice salah at home.

Ramadan

Ramadan is an important festival in the Islamic calendar, in which sawm (fasting) takes place. Ramadan is the name of the ninth month in the Islamic calendar, and lasts for either 29 or 30 days. During this time, those who participate in sawm may only eat before sunrise (suhur) and just after sunset (iftar). Like Easter, Ramadan doesn't occur at the same time each year, and is determined by the lunar cycle. It is marked by a crescent moon.

Most Muslims are expected to observe and participate in sawm during the month of Ramadan. However, there are a few exceptions:

Pregnant, breastfeeding, or menstruating women can be exempt from fasting during Ramadan.

Children are not expected to fast until they have reached twelve years of age. Elderly people are not expected to fast either if doing so could be detrimental to their health.

While it is not generally permitted to miss days of fasting, Muslims can make up those days at the end of Ramadan, or give food to the poor.

Muslims observe Ramadan for a number of reasons. Firstly, it is believed that some of the Qur'an was revealed to Muhammed during this month, giving it particular religious significance. However, it is also used to recognise how grateful one is to have food, and to discipline oneself.

The final day of Ramadan is called Id ul-Fitr, in which Muslims give thanks to Allah, exchange gifts, and end their fast. Prayer sessions are also held during this time. In addition, many Muslims donate money to charity as part of zakat.

Pilgrimage to Mecca

As mentioned in our section on the Five Pillars of Islam, pilgrimage to Mecca is an extremely important part of the Muslim faith. All Muslims are expected to travel to Mecca at least once in their life, provided that they can afford to and are in good enough physical health to do so. Muslims must make their pilgrimage during the twelfth month of the Islamic calendar, Dhu'l-Hijja.

Mecca is a holy place for a number of reasons. Firstly, Muhammed was born and lived there, making it an incredibly important site for Muslims. Additionally, it houses the Ka'aba: a giant cube made of stone. It is covered in a black cloth which has gold details on it. Some Muslims believe that the Ka'aba was created by Adam, whilst others believe it was Ibrahim and Isma'il. It is believed to have been designed as a place of worship. When Muslims pray as part of salah, they are praying towards Mecca and the Ka'aba, regardless of where they are in the world.

The Ka'aba is located inside Al-Masjid Al-Haram (The Sacred Mosque). Once Muslims arrive here, they must walk around the Ka'aba seven times in an anticlockwise motion. This is called tawaf, and pilgrims must wear simple white garments. This is to demonstrate that, before Allah, all humans are equal.

After visiting the Ka'aba, pilgrims then travel between the hills of Safa and Marwa. After this, they take water from the Zamzam Well. They then visit Mount Arafat, where they pray for forgiveness. They do this because this is the same site at which Adam prayed to God for forgiveness from being cast out of Eden. Muslims then collect stones at Muzdalifa, before throwing them at pillars in Mina. Muslims do this to drive the devil away.

Once they have completed their pilgrimage, Muslims are referred to as hajji.

JUDAISM

58 GCSE Religious Studies is Easy

The third major world religion we're going to be taking a look at in this guide is Judaism. In this chapter, we'll be looking at the following topics:

1. What is Judaism?
2. The Tenakh and Talmud.
3. Core beliefs in Judaism.
4. The key differences between Orthodox and Progressive Judaism.
5. Life, death, and the afterlife.
6. Sacred places and places of worship.
7. Festivals and worship.

What is Judaism?

Judaism is one of the three main Abrahamic religions, alongside Christianity and Judaism. It accepts the God of Abraham as its deity. It is also monotheistic: Judaism teaches that there is only one God, which is the God of the Old Testament.

While Judaism is a religion in the modern world, it is considered by many to be an ancient religion. This is because it was founded almost 3500 years ago. This makes it one of the oldest monotheistic religions, and also one of the oldest religions which still exists today. The religion was founded in the Middle-East, but has travelled around the entire world. As of 2015, there are approximately 15 million followers of Judaism in the world.

People who follow Judaism are referred to as Jews. Approximately 45% of the Jews in the world live in Israel, with another 45% living in America and Canada. The remaining 10% live in Europe, Asia, and Africa.

Judaism is founded on the covenant (contract) which Jews believe that God made with the Israelites in the Old Testament. Jews believe that the Israelites are God's chosen people, and that He specifically made a covenant with them, separating them from the many other religions which occurred at the time.

As you might have noticed, the Old Testament is being discussed quite frequently here. This is because Christianity is founded on Judaism –

Jesus was a Jew and his ministry related directly to Judaism. Christians and Jews both read the Old Testament, although there may be a few changes based on translation. Jewish teaching states a prophecy that a Messiah (saviour) will come to bring peace to the world. Christians believe that this Messiah was Jesus. Jews believe that Jesus was not the Messiah: the true Messiah is yet to come. This is the main reason why Judaism does not include the New Testament.

The Tenakh and Talmud

There are two main texts in Judaism. These are the Tenakh and the Talmud.

The Tenakh

The Tenakh is the primary text in Judaism. It's incredibly similar to Christianity's Old Testament, but you might find some changes due to translation. The main difference is that the Tenakh and the Old Testament are structured slightly differently to one another. The Tenakh is split into three major sections: the Torah, the Nevi'im, and the Ketuvim.

The Torah

The Torah is the first part of the Tenakh. It is made up of five books, which are also the first five books of the Christian Old Testament. These are:

1. Genesis.

2. Exodus.

3. Leviticus.

4. Numbers.

5. Deuteronomy.

These books cover many well-known stories, including the creation story, the flood, the freeing of the Israelites from Egypt, and more. This is also where the Commandments, known as the Mitzvot, appear. These books are also heavily focused on instructions, as Leviticus is full of laws which Jews are expected to follow. The word 'Torah' means 'instruction' or 'teaching'.

The Nevi'im
This part of the Tenakh recounts the stories of the prophets. These are divided into two groups: the Former Prophets and the Latter Prophets:

Former Prophets
1. Joshua.
2. Judges.
3. Samuel.
4. Kings.

These books begin after the death of Moses, and follow the prophets as they find Judaism and create Israel.

Latter Prophets
1. Isaiah.
2. Jeremiah.
3. Ezekiel.
4. The Twelve (minor prophets).

These later books follow the latter prophets, and focus less on storytelling and more on instruction and teaching.

The Ketuvim
This final book of the Tenakh focuses on teachings. This includes the following books:

The Three Poetic Books
1. Psalms.
2. Book of Proverbs.
3. Book of Job.

The Five Megillot
1. Song of Songs (also known as Song of Solomon).
2. Book of Ruth.
3. Lamentations.
4. Ecclesiastes.
5. Book of Esther.

Miscellaneous Books
1. Book of Daniel.

2. Book of Ezra.

3. Chronicles.

These books focus less on instructions and teaching, and more on poetry and revelation of the nature of God.

The Tenakh, and particularly the Torah, is treated with the utmost respect. During services at a synagogue, members of the community (congregation) will read passages from the Torah. The Torah is typically read in Hebrew, although there are translations to English and other languages available.

The Talmud
The Talmud is the second sacred text in Judaism. This text supplements the Tenakh, giving further guidance from scholars on how to interpret and follow the teachings of the Tenakh. This book is divided into two parts:

1. The Mishnah – This book gives further context for the laws in the Torah.

2. Gemara – This book is a commentary on the Mishnah.

Core Beliefs in Judaism
Like the other two major religions we've looked at, there's a number of core theological beliefs held in Judaism. These are fundamental to the Jewish faith, so it's important that you learn them before continuing!

The core beliefs we'll look at are:

1. The nature of God.

2. The covenant between God and the Israelites.

3. The Messiah and the Messianic Age.

4. The Mitzvot.

The Nature of God

Like Christians and Muslims, Jews believe that God possesses certain qualities. These are outlined in the Tenakh, and are as follows:

1. The One God – All Jews believe that God is the one true God. Unlike Christians, who believe in the Holy Trinity, Jews believe that God is irreducible: He is complete and cannot be divided into parts.

2. The Creator – Jews believe that God created the Heavens, the earth, and everything in between them.

3. Omnipotent – According to Judaism, God is all-powerful (omnipotent). This is how He was able to create everything, and how He can intervene in the world.

4. Omniscient – God is believed to know everything, or 'all-knowing'.

5. Omnibenevolent – God is all-loving and all-good, and is therefore incapable of sin.

6. Omnipresent – Jews believe that God exists in all places, at all times.

7. Eternal – Judaism teaches that God has always existed, and will always exist.

8. Immanent – Judaism teaches that, since God is everywhere, He participates and intervenes in the world. This concept is known as Shekhinah: God's presence on Earth.

9. Lawgiver – Jews believe that all of the laws in the Tenakh are given directly from God. If God says to do something, then we ought to do it!

10. Judge – Not only does God create the laws, He also judges how well people have followed them. This will result in people being sent to Heaven and Hell.

11. Merciful – While God is the judge, He will also be willing to forgive our sins.

12. Transcendent – Jews believe that God is beyond all other things. God exists beyond space and time, and is not limited to the logical or physical laws of our reality. God also exists independently of the universe – if the universe was somehow destroyed, God would continue to exist.

The Covenant Between God and the Israelites

An extremely important part of Judaism is the belief that God and the Israelites made a covenant. Jews believe that, during the time of the Old Testament, God and the Israelites entered a contract together. The agreement was that, so long as the Israelites worshipped and obeyed only Him, God would protect them and lead them to a promised land. For this reason, most Jews believe that Jews are God's chosen people.

God made two covenants with the Israelites. The first was with Abraham, who was led to Canaan by God and granted a son. Jews believe that Canaan was promised to Abraham, and therefore all Jews, by God.

The second covenant which Jews believe God made was with Moses during the Exodus. God sent plagues, and eventually the Angel of Death (believed to be Azrael), in order to force the Egyptians to free the Israelites, who were in slavery at the time. After this, God gave Moses the Ten Commandments at Mount Sinai, and then led them back to Canaan. In return for saving them, the Israelites made a promise to follow God's teachings and laws.

The Messiah and the Messianic Age

Like Christians, most Jews believe in the existence of a Messiah. Or, more accurately, Jews believe that a Messiah will one day exist, whilst Christians believe that the Messiah has already arrived (Jesus). Jews reject the notion that Jesus is the Messiah, and await the true Messiah's arrival.

Jews believe that the Messiah will begin an era of peace called the Messianic Age. Unlike Christians, who believe that Jesus was the Messiah and the son of God, Jews believe that the Messiah will not be divine-born. He will be a human, and a descendant of King David. Many Jews also believe that, during the Messianic Age, those who were good in life will be resurrected to enjoy it.

The Mitzvot

The Mitzvot are the laws in the Torah. These cover a range of different areas, from the preparation of food and how to maintain cleanliness, all the way to how to worship God. In total there are 613 Mitzvot. Don't worry, you don't need to know all of them for the exam!

Most of the Mitzvot are negative – they focus on telling Jews what they **should not** do. 365 of the Mitzvot are negative. The other 248

Mitzvot are positive – they tell Jews what they **should** do. Ten of the Mitzvot are the Ten Commandments, which are extremely important in Judaism.

Along with the Mitzvot, there are a number of other important teachings which Jews try to follow. These are:

1. Pikuach nefesh – This is the notion of preserving life. Jews are taught that preserving human life is incredibly important in Judaism.

2. Tikkun olam – This is the idea that Jews should be stewards of the world and its environments. This encourages many Jews to take environmentally-friendly action.

3. Acts of kindness – Jews are taught to be kind to one another, and to non-Jews as well.

The Key Differences Between Orthodox and Progressive Judaism

Judaism isn't one unified faith, and there are many different groups within Judaism. Here, we'll be taking a look at the differences between Orthodox Jews and Progressive Jews.

Orthodox Judaism
Orthodox Judaism is usually considered to be the stricter, more traditional form of Judaism. Orthodox Jews will attempt to follow all 613 of the Mitzvot as closely as possible, and will attempt to observe all of the other teachings in the Tenakh. Orthodox Jews will follow laws regarding the Shabbat (Sabbath), as well as laws regarding food and diet.

In addition, Orthodox Jews believe that the Tenakh and Talmud come directly from God. This means that they believe that the laws are immutable, and always apply. For this reason, Orthodox Jews tend to be more resistant to morality in the modern world, and refuse to reinterpret the Mitzvot to suit the modern world.

Progressive Judaism
Progressive Judaism is a lot more liberal in its teaching than Orthodox Judaism. Progressive Jews tend to not believe that the Tenakh and Talmud are the direct word of God, but are inspired by God. This means that the sacred texts are more open to interpretation.

Life, Death, and the Afterlife

The Afterlife
Unlike Christianity and Islam, which place great emphasis on reward and punishment in the afterlife, Judaism teaches that this life is where many will be rewarded or punished for their deeds. This means that many Jews try to live a good life for the sake of this life, rather than reward in the afterlife.

Despite this, many Jews believe that, in the Messianic Age, God will judge everyone. Those who are deemed to have lived good lives are believed to be resurrected and join with God and the Messiah in the Messianic Age. Those who have lived in sin without repentance will be punished.

Another belief about life after death involves Eden (Paradise) and Gehinnom (Hell). Many Jews believe that most souls will go to Gehinnom – some permanently, and some only temporarily. This is similar to the Catholic doctrine of purgatory, which teaches that many will spend time in a temporary Hell before being purged and allowed to enter Heaven.

Orthodox Jews tend to believe that their physical forms will be resurrected during the Messianic Age. For this reason, Orthodox Jews do not allow for any practices which damage the body after death, such as autopsies or cremations. Progressive Jews who believe in the Messianic Age tend to believe that their souls will be resurrected instead. Therefore, the body has less significance after death.

Jewish Dietary Laws
A well-known part of Judaism is its laws regarding diet and the preparation of food. These laws are known as the kashrut. Food that is permitted by these laws are called 'kosher', whilst everything else is 'trefah'.

Here are some qualifications that food, particularly meat, has to meet in order to be kosher:

1. Jews are not permitted to eat blood. Therefore, the animal must be entirely drained of blood before the meat can be prepared and eaten.

2. Mammals may only be eaten if they have cloven hooves and chew

cud. This means that cows (beef) may be eaten, but pigs (pork) cannot.

3. The only seafood that can be eaten must have fins and scales. This means that food such as prawns, lobsters, and squid are not kosher.

4. Poultry, such as chicken, is kosher.

Sacred Places and Places of Worship

Like most world religions, Judaism has a number of sacred sites and places of worship. Let's take a look at those now.

The Synagogue
The synagogue is the main place of worship for Jews. Jews attend the synagogue for group prayer sessions, study groups, celebration of events, and generally to meet as a community.

Temple Mount
Temple Mount is a hill in the Old City of Jerusalem. Judaism teaches that God's divine presence is most prominent here, making it the most holy site in all of Judaism. Due to restrictions, most Jews are not able to stand on Temple Mount itself, and instead pray at the Western Wall. Jerusalem in general is considered to be the holiest city in Judaism.

Festivals and Worship

There's a number of different festivals and forms of worship in Judaism. It's important that you learn these carefully.

Shabbat (Sabbath)
The Shabbat is the Jewish day of rest, which begins just before sunset on Friday night, and ends after the appearance of three stars in the sky on Saturday night. Almost all Jews observe the Shabbat, although the practices on this day differ.

Generally speaking, Jews are not permitted to work on the Shabbat. Orthodox Jews are stricter on this teaching, whilst Progressive Jews might allow for some work to be completed. The Shabbat is observed to remember the day on which God rested after creating the world.

Passover

Passover, also known as Pesach, is the celebration of the Passover event in the Old Testament. This was when Moses commanded the Israelites, enslaved by the Egyptians, to paint blood on their doors and prepare to escape from Egypt. Jews (and Christians) believe that, on that night, the angel of death flew over Egypt and killed the first-born son of every Egyptian family. After this happened, the Israelites were able to flee from Egypt.

Jews believe that on that night, the Israelites ate unleavened bread (bread without yeast) because they had no time to wait for the bread to rise. During the 7-8 day festival of Passover, Jews eat specific food to commemorate the event.

Rosh Hashanah

Rosh Hashanah is the Jewish New Year. It occurs sometime in September or October, and focuses on reflection and introspection. Jews are expected to think carefully about their actions in the past year, and look forward to the next year to see how they can improve.

Yom Kippur

In the Jewish calendar, Yom Kippur is the day of atonement. This is the holiest day in the Jewish year. Jews pray to God to have their sins forgiven. On this day, Jews are not permitted to work. Additionally, Jews are expected to fast for 25 hours.

Brit Milah

This is a ceremony which usually takes place 7 days after the birth of a boy. Almost all boys in the Jewish faith are circumcised at part of Brit Milah. This is performed by a specialist known as a mohel. Blessings are said before the procedure, and is followed by the boy having been given his Hebrew name.

Simchat Bat

This is the naming ceremony in which baby girls are welcomed into a family, Jewish community, and the Jewish faith. This is when the girl will receive a Hebrew name.

Bar/Bat Mitzvah

This is a coming of age ceremony for boys and girls in the Jewish faith. For boys, this ceremony occurs at age thirteen, in which the boy becomes 'bar mitzvah'. For girls, this occurs at age 12, and the girl becomes 'bat mitzvah'. 'Bar/Bat Mitzvah' means 'Son/Daughter of the Commandments.'

UNIT 2: RELIGION IN PRACTICE

THE EXISTENCE OF GOD

One of the most heated debates throughout human history has focused on the existence of god. Since the three religions we have discussed are completely dependent on the existence of their respective god, it's understandable that defending the existence of god is one of the most important areas of debate for many religious people. After all, if god does not exist, then it follows that:

1. Religious texts hold no significance over any other book, since they would not be the word of god.

2. The objective morality commanded by these religious texts would not objective at all.

Additionally, if god is not real, then it's probable (although not necessarily true) that there is no afterlife either.

For this reason, theologians and other philosophers throughout the ages have taken up proverbial arms and attempted to defend their faith through argument. Arguments for the existence of god include:

1. **The teleological argument** – the argument that god must exist because there is evidence that the universe and its inhabitants were intelligently designed.

2. **The cosmological argument** – the claim that there must be a 'first cause' which kick-started everything in reality. Religious apologists and theologians have argued that God is this first cause.

3. **The ontological argument** – an argument which states that, since God exists as an idea, and because God is the most powerful being, then God must exist.

4. **The moral argument** – an argument which claims that, in spite of human morality contradicting the rules of nature, humans still often choose to be moral. This morality must come from God.

The two key arguments that you need to know are the teleological (design) argument, and the cosmological (first cause) argument.

The Design Argument

The universe, and everything within it, is incredibly intricate. From insects to galaxies, every single part of nature is incredibly complex, with lots of different systems working to keep things in a state of order. For many religious people, this demonstrates that there is a divine being which created and maintains the universe. In other words, the universe has been designed by something which we might consider to be a god.

In order to prove their point, supporters of the design argument will point to lots of things in nature. For example, supporters of the design argument might claim that, because the human eye is so complex and intricate, it would be impossible for it to be created by anything other than an intelligent being.

The other angle of the design argument examines how everything appears to be designed with a purpose. For example, the human eye has the purpose of allowing us to see, and every other organ in our bodies also fulfils a function of some kind. Supporters of the design argument often claim that, since everything in the universe has some kind of purpose, there must be a divine creator who has decided on what that purpose might be.

Who Supports the Design Argument?
The design argument is not limited to any single religion. In fact, Jewish, Muslim, and Christian theologians have all supported design arguments of some kind. The exact details of their arguments might differ in places, but all seem to agree that the complexity and apparent purpose of the universe and its parts means that there must be a creator at work. Since this creator would have to be extremely powerful in order to design the entire universe, it is believed that the creator is God.

Counter-Arguments to the Design Argument
Since the design argument has been frequently used by religious apologists, it has also been met with a lot of counter-arguments and criticisms. These include:

1. The complexity of the world does not imply a designer, especially when other explanations exist. For example, evolutionary theory shows us that organs and organisms develop gradually over millions of years. This means that there might not be a god designing everything!

2. Just because it looks like there might be purpose, this doesn't mean that there actually is any in the universe. Even if things do have purpose, that doesn't mean that the purpose was designed

by God. For example, the purpose of most organisms, according to evolutionary theory, is to preserve their genetic material and reproduce. This is a purpose designated by nature, not necessarily by God!

3. While it might seem that the universe is in a state of order, this isn't necessarily the case. The cosmos is often incredibly chaotic, with cataclysmic events frequently occurring throughout space. This means that there might not be as much order in the universe as we think!

The First Cause Argument

This argument, sometimes known as the cosmological argument, focuses less on the complex details of the universe, and more on the existence of the universe itself.

First, it is assumed that something cannot come from nothing, nor can something create itself. This means that the universe cannot have created itself, nor could it have come into being from nothingness. In addition, we know that an event occurred at the start of the universe called the big bang. This means that the universe has not always existed.

If the universe has not always existed, then something must have created it. Since something cannot create itself, the universe did not create itself. Likewise, since something cannot come from nothing, the universe was not created out of nothing. Therefore, something else must have created the universe. Something might have created the universe, but this too must have been created by something else. This creates an infinite regress of causes, and therefore there must be a cause which began everything else.

In other words, there had to be a 'first cause' which kick-started all of reality. Supporters of the first cause argument believe that this first cause is God, because he is eternal and all-powerful.

Who Supports the First Cause Argument?

The first cause argument is supported by scholars and members of many world religions. St. Thomas Aquinas, an incredibly influential 13th Century Christian scholar, formulated a version of the cosmological argument which is still supported to this day. Likewise, the Muslim scholar al-Ghazali theorised a similar first cause argument, which

THE EXISTENCE OF GOD

states that Allah is the first cause which started the universe.

The first cause argument for the existence of a god or multiple gods can apply to any religion or worldview which accepts the following principles:

The universe, reality, or whatever contains reality must have started at some point (i.e. it can't be eternal).

There must be a God which is eternal and incredibly powerful.

In other words, you must believe that God pre-dates the origins of the universe.

Counter-Arguments to the First Cause Argument
Here are a few refutations of the first-cause argument, which include:

1. In order to accept the first cause argument, you must already accept that there is an all-powerful and eternal god. If you don't believe in God, you might be happy to accept the infinite regress.

2. As the cosmological argument states, nothing can create itself. So, what created God? Why is it that God can be eternal, but the universe cannot?

The Existence of Miracles
A miracle is an event or occurrence which cannot be explained by scientific understanding, or something which appears to break the laws of nature in some way. Miracles are a central part of many religions, since the existence of miracles demonstrates the existence of a higher power, and how that higher power is involved in the world.

Christianity and Miracles
All Christians believe that at least one miracle occurred: the resurrection of Jesus Christ. This is a miracle because Jesus rose from the dead, which contradicts everything we know about nature. This miracle shows not only that Jesus is the son of God, but also that there is an afterlife. Therefore, it's one of the most important (if not **the** most important) part of Christian teaching.

However, this wasn't the only miracle which supposedly took place. According to all of the four gospels, Jesus performed miracles to demonstrate that he was the son of God, but also to help others. Most of his miracles involve healing the sick or helping the poor, but others include turning water into wine, and walking on water.

Miracles are especially important to the Catholic Church because, in order to become a saint, you must have been witness to at least two miracles. For example, Thomas Aquinas was canonised (made into a Saint) because he supposedly witnessed 'salted fish' turning into herrings while on his death bed.

While some Christians only believe that miracles occurred during the time of Jesus Christ, there are others who believe that miracles still happen today. An example of a 'modern miracle' would be the Toronto Blessing, in which over 300 visitors to an evangelical church in Toronto, Canada claimed to have miraculously received gold and silver tooth fillings.

Islam and Miracles
Miracles are also an important part of Islam. For instance, many Muslims believe that the Qur'an is, in itself, a miracle. This is because it is believed that, without Allah's guidance, it would be impossible to copy the Qur'an (Qur'an 17:88). This is reinforced by the fact that the Qur'an discusses scientific ideas such as the big bang long before these phenomena are accounted for scientifically. Some Muslims believe that this is evidence that the Qur'an is the word of Allah, since it contains information which pre-dates scientific discovery.

Similar to Jesus, many Muslims are of the belief that the prophets performed miracles. Like Jesus, these miracles demonstrated that the prophets were messengers of God, rather than false prophets or liars.

Judaism and Miracles
Miracles also occur frequently in the Torah. One such example of a miracle occurs when God turns the water in the Nile to blood, making it undrinkable for the Egyptians holding the Israelites in slavery.

While miracles are a part of Jewish doctrine, individual miracles aren't as significant in the faith as they are for Christianity. Instead, Judaism places greater emphasis on creation and life as a whole being a miracle.

THE EXISTENCE OF GOD

Miracles as Proof that God Exists
For many religious people, miracles prove two things:

God exists, because without God, there would be no way to suspend or break the laws of nature.

God takes an active role in His creation. The fact that God performs miracles in the world shows that he tends to His creation, and is not a distant god.

Remember that belief in miracles isn't always a necessary part of religious belief. Some Christians, Jews, and Muslims might find some miracles to be important, but instead focus on the miracles teaching a moral message or a message about God.

Counter-Arguments to Miracles
If you do not believe in gods, or any other supernatural occurrences, then you will likely find it hard to believe that the laws of nature can be bent or broken. David Hume, an 18th Century philosopher, argued that it is more likely that we are *mistaken* about the laws or nature when we perceive a miracle, rather than the laws of nature actually being broken. For example, it might appear as though someone's disease was cured by God, when in fact it might just be the placebo effect working in the patient.

Exam-Style Questions
Here are some questions you could be asked in your exam. The answers to these questions can be found in this chapter, so make sure you're able to answer all of them before moving on!

1. Give two religious beliefs about miracles. (2 marks)
2. Explain how design proves that God exists. (4 marks)
3. Give two religious beliefs about the design argument. (2 marks)
4. Explain how scientific theories might relate to religious belief about the existence of God. (4 marks)
5. "Religious people do not need to prove the existence of God. They should accept it on faith." Evaluate this statement. (12 marks)

RELIGION AND THE WORLD

For many religious people, past and present, religion is about much more than telling us what to do and what not to do. In fact, for thousands of years, religion played a fundamental role in helping to explain the universe and life around us. With the emergence of science, religion's explanatory importance has lessened, but is still noteworthy since so many people found their beliefs about the world on religious doctrine. In this chapter, we will be taking a look at the following areas:

- Religion and the environment;
- Religion and the universe;
- Abortion and euthanasia.

Christianity, Islam, and Judaism all teach on these areas. We'll be taking a look at each, as well as what these three religions have to say about them.

Religion and the Environment

Something that the three Abrahamic religions (Christianity, Islam, and Judaism) have in common is the idea of stewardship. By this, it is meant that human beings have the God-given responsibility to look after the planet and its environment.

Earth's environment has clearly been affected by human activity. The industrialisation of the world (creation of factories and mass-produced goods) has resulted in pollution around the world. Deforestation has caused some species of animal to become extinct. Our reliance on fossil fuels such as petrol have damaged the earth's atmosphere – potentially permanently. As the most intelligent beings on the planet, and with the most influence over Earth's environmental future, it doesn't take a religious person to want to protect the world from further environmental damage. One thing that the following religions have in common is that they all accept that the earth was created by God out of love for His creation. Therefore, to ruin the earth is to reject one of God's greatest gifts to us.

Let's take a look at what Christianity, Islam, and Judaism have to say about the environment and humanity's place in it.

Christianity and the Environment

Genesis, the first book of the Bible, states that humans are given dominion over the earth, and are to rule over the other animals which inhabit the earth. This seems to suggest that humans are allowed to do whatever they want with the world, which is partially true: many Christians believe that God gave us free will so we could make decisions for ourselves. However, just because we can ruin the environment, doesn't mean that we should. In Genesis, God sets Adam and Eve to work as caretakers in Eden. Whether you believe that the creation story is literally true or not doesn't matter here, since the message is that Christians should take care of the environment.

Christian organisations such as CAFOD work on the principles of stewardship, attempting to look after the environment as well as the humans who inhabit it.

Islam and the Environment
Like Christians, Muslims believe that the planet is a gift from Allah. Therefore, it should be treated with respect. In the Qur'an, the Prophet Muhammed stated that it is good to plant trees. For many Muslims, this shows that taking care of the environment is an important part of the Muslim faith.

Like Christians, Muslims tend to believe that human beings are stewards of the earth, or 'Khalifah', which means trustee. Muslims believe that Allah has entrusted the world to us, which in turn means that it is our responsibility to take care of it. Many Muslims also believe that Allah will judge how well we cared for the environment on judgement day.

Judaism and the Environment
Since Genesis is also a book in the Torah, Jews also believe that God gave humans dominion over the earth and its contents. Additionally, Jews tend to believe that human beings are stewards of the earth. Since the planet is a gift from God, we should take care of it out of respect and love for Him.

The Jewish concept of 'tikkun olam' ('mending the world') extends to protection of the environment. In order to help mend the world, we need to take care of the things which allow it to continue existing, such as the atmosphere, trees, and oceans!

Religion and the Universe
The universe is the place in which the entirety of our reality exists. As you can imagine, that makes it rather important for all of the major

religions!

The first thing to remember is that Judaism, Christianity, and Islam all hold the believe that there is more out there than just the universe. Heaven and Hell, for example, are not believed to exist inside the universe. This means that, when we die, most faiths believe that our souls leave the universe. That said, religions still have a lot to say about the universe we live in!

The current scientific consensus for the origins of the universe is that, billions and billions of years ago, the entirety of the universe was condensed into a miniscule point. Then, this point exploded, giving birth to the universe. This is what is known as the big bang. Over time, the universe has continued to change and expand, populated with a seemingly countless number of stars, planets, and galaxies.

When it comes to the origins of life, the scientific view is that all creatures on Earth, and probably the entire universe, developed slowly over time. When life on Earth was in its early stages, lifeforms would have been incredibly simple and tiny. As these creatures reproduced, random changes in their genetic material would have created new traits. The creatures with traits which helped them survive would go on to reproduce, and over time more traits would develop. Eventually, the microorganisms from millions of years ago would evolve into the animals that we have today – including human beings! This process is known as evolution by natural selection.

While these scientific explanations for the origins of the universe and life are accepted by many, religions still maintain their own beliefs about life and the universe's beginnings. Sometimes, these beliefs are complementary to scientific understanding. In other cases, they are directly contradictory. Let's take a look at what Christianity, Islam, and Judaism have to say about the origins of life and the universe.

Christianity and the Universe
According to Genesis, everything was created by God in six days. If taken literally, this directly contradicts the scientific facts about the universe: it took billions of years to get to where we are now, not six days!

Some Christians take everything in the Bible literally. Known as 'literalists' or 'fundamentalists', these Christians genuinely believe that

God created the world in six days, which usually means that they do not believe in evolution or the big bang. Some of these Christians go a step further, and argue that the scientific evidence for evolution and the big bang are incomplete. Therefore, these theories cannot be trusted.

However, not all Christians literally interpret Genesis. Many Christians see it as symbolic: the exact details of how God created the world aren't important. Instead, what's important is what the story tells us about God. For example, the creation story in Genesis shows that God created human beings in His image and likeness. You might not have to literally accept the details of the story to accept that humans are special and created by God.

Interestingly, many great scientists and philosophers have attempted to bridge the gap between religion and science throughout history. Isaac Newton, for example, used his understanding of the solar system to try and find out the precise date when Jesus was born!

Ultimately, there is no single accepted way of interpreting the creation story in Genesis. Some Christians believe that God literally created the world in six days, which means that the big bang and evolution are not true. Other Christians believe that the creation story is symbolic, and therefore their Christian beliefs about God and scientific consensus can co-exist.

Islam and the Universe
The creation story in the Qur'an is not too different from that of the Torah and Bible. According to the Qur'an, Allah created the heavens and the earth in six days. Likewise, Allah created human beings out of clay, and then breathed life into them.

Like Christians, Muslims hold diverse beliefs about how their creation story interacts with the scientific theories about the origins of life. Some Muslims will adopt a literalist stance, stating that the events in the creation story literally occurred. On the other hand, some Muslims might read the creation story as symbolic.

Judaism and the Universe
The creation story in the Torah is mostly similar to the Christian creation story. Some Jews, such as ultra-orthodox Jews, will read Genesis literally. Other Jews will opt for a more symbolic interpretation of Genesis.

Religion, Abortion, and Euthanasia

While religions have a lot to say about the universe and the environment, they also have a lot of beliefs about life itself. Christianity, Judaism, and Islam all have doctrines which impact whether or not they accept abortion and euthanasia as moral actions. Before continuing, lets take a look at what abortion and euthanasia are.

Abortion

Abortion is the act of terminating (or aborting) a pregnancy, resulting in the death of the foetus that is being carried by the pregnant woman. Generally speaking, abortion comes in two forms:

1. **Medical abortion** – this process usually occurs earlier in the pregnancy. The pregnant takes a pill or other kind of medicine which causes an abortion.

2. **Surgical abortion** – this process involves some kind of intrusive surgery, which removes the foetus from the woman's body and results in termination of the pregnancy. This process usually involves using some kind of suction or vacuum technology to remove the foetus from the woman's womb.

Both these forms of abortion are legal in England, Scotland, and Wales. Medical abortions are used up to the ninth week of pregnancy, whilst surgical abortions are used from the ninth week up to the twenty-fourth week. Abortions are legal in most circumstances up until the twenty-fourth week of the pregnancy. After the twenty-fourth week, abortions are not permitted.

There are two exceptions to this rule, however. The first is in the case where the pregnancy threatens the life of the pregnant woman. In this case, termination of the pregnancy can occur up to just before the point of birth.

The second exception is in the case where it is believed that the foetus will be severely disabled after birth. In this case, the pregnant woman reserves the right to abort the pregnancy up to the day before birth.

Since abortion results in the death of the foetus, it is incredibly controversial – especially among religious groups. Someone who is against abortion is usually described as being "pro-life", whilst someone in favour of women having a right to an abortion are often called "pro-choice".

Christianity and Abortion

Christians believe that humans are made in God's image and likeness, and that life is a gift from God. Therefore, to take a life, even the life of a foetus, would be wasting God's gift.

In addition, one of the Ten Commandments is "thou shalt not kill". Many Christians believe that life begins at conception (when the embryo is first created after sexual intercourse). Therefore, abortion is a form of killing.

In addition, Genesis states that God wishes for us to be 'fruitful and multiply' – we should reproduce. Having an abortion is the exact opposite of being fruitful and multiplying.

In most cases, Christians oppose abortion in the majority of circumstances. Many churches, such as the Catholic Church, are formally opposed to abortion in almost all situations. The only exception that is accepted by most churches is in cases where the pregnancy might threaten the life of the mother. In the Catholic Church, this is known as the doctrine of double-effect.

The Catholic and Protestant Churches often propose that, rather than having an abortion, pregnant women should consider putting unwanted children up for adoption.

Islam and Abortion

Generally speaking, Islamic teaching is that abortion is morally wrong. The Qur'an makes it very clear that killing is wrong. So, if you believe that foetus' are living human beings, then killing them must be wrong.

The Qur'an directly speaks about the killing of children, saying that it is a great sin. Many Muslims believe this to include unborn children (i.e. foetuses and embryos).

While Christians often believe that human life begins at conception, the Qur'an teaches that 'ensoulment', the point at which human life is given a soul, occurs 120 days after conception (approximately four months). This has led some Muslims to believe that abortion is permissible in cases where the pregnant woman's life is at risk, or if the child will be born with a severe disability or birth defect, provided that the abortion takes place within the first 120 days.

Judaism and Abortion

Like Christianity and Islam, Judaism generally teaches that abortion is wrong. Life is a gift from God, so to abort a foetus is to reject God's gift of life. Since the Ten Commandments are part of Jewish teaching, then Judaism teaches that killing is wrong. Abortion is arguably a form of killing a human life, which means that it goes against God's word.

However, Judaism does not teach that life begins at conception. Therefore, the foetus is only considered a human when it is born. This means that Jews can permit abortion in some circumstances.

Euthanasia

Euthanasia is the act of ending someone's life, usually because they are in some position of suffering. For example, if someone suffered from a terminal illness that was extremely painful, they might ask to be euthanised to spare them the suffering, and to give themselves a dignified death.

The word 'euthanasia' roughly translates from Ancient Greek to mean 'a good death'. When someone requests to be euthanised, they are usually not in a position to take their own life, such as in the case of a quadriplegic – someone is who paralysed from the neck down. Since this person is incapable of taking their own life, they might wish for someone else to help them do so.

Euthanasia is currently illegal in the United Kingdom, but is legal in some other parts of the world.

Christianity and Euthanasia

The Christian teaching on euthanasia is somewhat split. Since euthanasia involves killing, and killing goes against the Ten Commandments, then euthanasia must also go against God's will. However, some Christians recognise that there is a difference between murder and euthanasia. Some Christians believe that "thou shalt not kill" was more focused on saying that murder was immoral, whilst euthanasia often involves consent on the part of the individual who wishes to die. For this reason, some Christians believe that euthanasia is acceptable in some circumstances.

Some Christians believe that passive euthanasia, when inaction results in death rather than action, is permissible. One case of this might be if life-supporting medicine is taken away from the patient, rather than actively injecting them with a lethal chemical. Some Christians believe that this is acceptable because you aren't making an action. However, others believe that this is a sin of omission, since your inaction is resulting in death.

Other Christians are completely opposed to euthanasia. Some Christians believe that it is not up to us to decide when we die, but rather it is all part of God's plan. Some Christians believe that suffering is an essential part of life, and that we must endure it in order to enter heaven. After all, we accept God's blessings – why don't we accept life's troubles as well?

Islam and Euthanasia
Generally speaking, Muslims are against euthanasia. This is mainly because the Qur'an teaches that Allah has a plan for each and every one of us. In some cases, suffering is part of that plan, and to exercise euthanasia is a means of subverting Allah's will.

In cases where the patient has no signs of improving and is in extreme pain, palliative care (such as painkillers) are approved of rather than euthanasia.

Judaism and Euthanasia
Like Christianity and Islam, Judaism is mostly opposed to euthanasia. This is because Jews believe that only God can say when people die. God is almighty, and we are His creation. Therefore, God is the only one who gets to decide when we live and die. For this reason, euthanasia is acting against His will.

The Jewish concept of pikuach nefesh states that we should only act to save and preserve human lives. We should never act in a way which ends life. Since euthanasia results in the death of the patient, it goes against pikuach nefesh.

Like Christianity, some Jews believe that passive euthanasia is acceptable. This is when treatment is withheld, which brings about the patient's death. This is considered to be preferable to active euthanasia, which would entail actively giving the patient some kind of chemical which resulted in their death.

Exam-Style Questions

Here are some questions you could be asked in your exam. The answers to these questions can be found in this chapter, so make sure you're able to answer all of them before moving on!

1. Which of the three major religions believes in ensoulment? (1 mark)

2. Explain two similar religious beliefs about euthanasia. (2 marks)

3. Explain why Christians generally believe that abortion is a sin. (4 marks)

4. Explain the difference between medical and surgical abortion. (4 marks)

5. "Abortion should never be allowed, under any circumstances." Evaluate this statement. (12 marks)

RELIGION AND RELATIONSHIPS

Relationships, particularly sexual ones, are a huge part of our lives. Therefore, religion has a lot of teachings about sex, sexuality, marriage, and more. In this chapter, we'll be taking a look at what Christianity, Islam, and Judaism have to say about the following areas:

- Sex and Sexuality;
- Contraception;
- Marriage and Divorce.

Religion, Sex, and Sexuality

Religious Attitudes Towards Sex

Sex and sexuality are an inescapable part of humanity, and religions have a lot to say about them both. After all, sex is what we do in order to reproduce, something which Christianity, Islam, and Judaism teach that we should do. Because these three religions primarily associate sex with procreation (having children), the teachings on sex and relationships are quite specific, and in some cases are extremely strict.

Most Christian, Islamic, and Jewish doctrines share the same teachings on sex. Sex is an act which is only considered to be moral in the correct context. Generally, this means that sex is only considered to be morally acceptable when it takes place within marriage, with the purpose to have children.

For example, the Catholic Church teaches that sex is a unitive act, and should only occur between a married man and his wife. Sex consummates a marriage – it binds the husband and wife together in an intimate way. In addition, the Catholic Church teaches that sex is a procreative act, and should only be performed in order to have children. This means that the Catholic Church has traditionally opposed contraception (see the next section for information about religion and contraception).

These three religions are uniformly against adultery (having sex with a married person who you are not married to, or having sex while married, but not to your spouse) and fornication (sex outside of marriage). The Qur'an states that those who seek sex outside of marriage are transgressors, while the Old Testament and Torah regularly state that adultery is a sin (such as in the Ten Commandments).

To summarise, Christians, Muslims, and Jews tend to believe the following things about sex:

1. Sex should only occur within marriage because it makes sex more special and also binds a husband and wife together in a spiritual way.

2. Sex should primarily take place when procreation is the primary goal.

3. Sex with someone you are not married to, or having sex with a married person, is considered immoral.

Religious Attitudes Towards Sexuality

While the three religions we've looked at all share a similar stance towards sex, sexuality is where things get a bit more complicated. By sexuality, we mean sexual orientation, such as homosexuality (being attracted to members of the same sex). Officially, homosexuality has traditionally been considered immoral, although many world religions and their members have felt the pressure of homosexuality being more accepted in modern society.

Traditionally, the Catholic Church has completely opposed homosexuality. However, the stance of the Church has changed in more recent times, placing a greater emphasis on the act of homosexual sex rather than homosexuality itself. The Catholic Church accepts homosexual people, and states that they should not be discriminated against. However, the Catholic Church believes that homosexuals should not act on their desires (i.e. have homosexual sex). Therefore, the Catholic Church seems to adopt the stance that being homosexual isn't a sin, but acting on one's homosexuality is.

Other Christian churches are more liberal (accepting) when it comes to homosexuality. Some of the Church of England's clergy are gay, and many within the Church of England accept homosexuality. Other churches, such as some extreme evangelical churches, believe that homosexuality of all kinds is a sin.

Christian, Jewish, and Muslim sacred texts all seem to condemn homosexual acts. For example, Leviticus states that it is sinful for men to sleep with other men, and all three sacred texts state that God destroyed the city of Sodom because it was populated with those who engaged in homosexual sex. Some religious people believe that, since these texts were written in a very different time to the current era, their teachings on homosexuality are outdated and should change.

Religion and Contraception

Contraception is the act of preventing a pregnancy from occurring. There are two kinds of contraception:

1. **Natural contraception** – This occurs when the couple use methods which do not involve man-made products such as condoms or contraceptive pills. An example of contraception would be to only have sex during times of the menstrual cycle when the woman is least likely to become pregnant.

2. **Artificial contraception** – This is the use of artificial or man-made products to prevent pregnancy, such as the contraceptive pill, contraceptive implant, or a condom.

On top of this, there are temporary and permanent forms of contraception. For example, a condom is a form of temporary contraception, whilst sterilisation (a procedure which prevents someone from being able to have children) is permanent contraception.

Different religions and denominations have varying attitudes towards contraception.

Christianity and Contraception

Since the Catholic Church primarily views sex as a means of procreation, it teaches that practices which unnaturally prevent pregnancy (or terminate it, in the case of abortion) are immoral. The Catholic Church has historically taught against artificial contraception such as condoms and the contraceptive pill.

The Catholic Church states that any method of 'deliberate' contraception is morally wrong. This means that there is room in the Catholic Church's teaching to allow for means of natural contraception.

While the Catholic Church as an institution teaches that artificial contraception is wrong, this is a controversial issue among many Catholics. Many argue that the Catholic Church's stance towards condoms means that some Catholic countries in the world are not able to combat sexually transmitted infections. For example, the rejection of condoms in some African countries has arguably led to an increase in HIV.

The Catholic Church believes that the liberal use of contraception promotes sexual promiscuity and fornication. In turn, this makes sex less meaningful between two married people.

Other Christian churches are divided on contraception. Many Protestant Churches are in favour of contraception because the Bible does not directly teach on the matter, and because artificial contraception can be used for the purpose of family planning.

Some Christians might even argue that, if people are allowed to use artificial contraception, they are less likely to have an unwanted pregnancy and resort to abortion.

Islam and Contraception
Unlike Catholicism, Islam does not have a singular teaching when it comes to contraception. Some Muslims believe that contraception, both natural and artificial, are a force for good because they allow families to plan effectively. This can result in circumstances such as where additional children would be a burden on the family.

Some Muslims believe that contraception is wrong because, if a woman becomes pregnant, this is Allah's will. This means that some Muslims accept natural contraception, but not artificial contraception. Other Muslims who accept both forms of contraception see them as a temporary measure. For this reason, permanent forms of contraception like sterilisation are not permitted.

Judaism and Contraception
Jewish teaching on contraception stems from the same passages of the Old Testament as it does for Catholicism and Christianity. In Genesis, we are told to be fruitful and multiply. Since contraception prevents children from being conceived, most Orthodox Jews do not accept contraception in most circumstances.

Similar to Islam, some Jews find contraception to be acceptable so long as it is used for family planning. So, if a married couple use it in order to plan when they want to have children, this is acceptable. However, this married couple is expected to have children, and therefore some Jews would find it unacceptable to use temporary measures with no intention of having children in the future.

Other Jews think that it is up to each individual to decide on whether they want to use contraception.

Religion, Marriage, and Divorce

Marriage

While the practice dates back for thousands of years, marriage is still a significant part of our culture. However, less and less people are getting married in the modern era, particularly in the UK. In addition, the number of divorces is still much more frequent than it was even fifty years ago.

There have been other changes to marriage laws in the UK which have had a significant impact on religious teachings about marriage. Same-sex marriage (i.e. two men getting married, or two women getting married) has been legal in England, Wales, and Scotland since 2014. Northern Ireland does not recognise or practice same-sex marriage. These changes both in law and culture have had an impact on how religions deal with marriage.

Marriage is a fundamental part of many world religions. The practice of marriage itself is mostly a religious concept: the combining of two people in the eyes of God. While many non-religious people also choose to marry, marriage plays a vital role in many religions. Let's take a look at what Christianity, Islam, and Judaism teach about marriage.

Christianity and Marriage

The Bible teaches Christians that marriage is a holy process. Therefore, many Christians regard marriage as a fundamentally important part of faith. Marriage is the act of making a covenant (promise or contract) between two people in the presence of God.

The purpose of marriage is to love one another and to love God together, but also to create a household and environment suitable to raise children in. Since many Christians believe that children should only be born to married couples, and because procreation is an important part of Christian faith, then it follows that marriage is extremely important for Christians who intend to have children.

Moreover, most Christians believe that being faithful to one's spouse is of utmost important. To commit adultery is a sin, as listed in the Ten Commandments. Therefore, rejection of adultery is universal in the Christian faith – it is not restricted to a single denomination.

Some Christian faiths do not accept cohabitation (two romantically-involved people living together before being married). However, this is a doctrine that has become less and less accepted in the modern era, since financial difficulty and modern housing and rental markets meaning it is more practical for people to live together before they marry.

Same-sex marriage is an issue which affects all Christian denominations. Some churches, such as the Catholic Church and Church of England, believe that allowing homosexuals to marry might degrade the sanctity of marriage. Their argument is that marriage is special and should only occur between a man and a woman in the eyes of God – just as the Bible details it.

Just because church leaders reject same-sex marriage, does not mean that their congregations agree with them. Many individual Christians believe that same-sex marriage is a part of the modern world, and that the church needs to adapt to the times.

Islam and Marriage
Like Christianity, marriage is an important part of life for many Muslims. In the Qur'an, Muslims are told to "marry the unmarried among you" (Qur'an 24:32). Muslims believe that marriage is a gift from Allah, and therefore should be undertaken as a way of respecting Him and enacting His will.

Muslims believe that marriage is important because it helps to create a suitable environment for procreation – another extremely important part of the Muslim faith.

Adultery is considered to be a sin in the Muslim faith, and it is often taken very seriously. In addition, sex outside of marriage is considered to be sinful, and therefore cohabitation is often not accepted by Muslims.

In the United Kingdom, Muslims often need to have two separate ceremonies in order to get married. For their marriage to be recognised by the State, Muslims must have a civil ceremony. On top of this, Muslims will have an Islamic wedding ceremony, known as Nikah.

Since many Muslims believe that homosexual acts are sinful, many Muslims also believe that same-sex marriage is immoral. Instead, many Muslims suggest that gay couples have civil partnerships instead. In addition, a lot of Muslims believe that, because the purpose of marriage is to have children, then same-sex marriages are immoral.

However, there are many Muslims who support same-sex marriage. These Muslims argue that, since marriage is an important part of the Muslim faith, homosexual Muslims should be allowed to partake in it as well, even if they can't naturally have children.

Judaism and Marriage
Like Christianity and Islam, marriage is an important aspect of the Jewish faith. It's a process which binds a couple together in the eyes of God – a physical and spiritual bonding.

God created Eve to be Adam's companion in Genesis. Many Jews see this as evidence that God wants us to marry. Like Christianity and Islam, marriage is a holy event – the name of the wedding ceremony is kiddushin, which roughly translates to sanctification.

Orthodox Jews tend to reject cohabitation because it invites the possibility of sexual relationships outside of wedlock. Progressive Jews, however, are much more liberal on this matter.

One aspect of Judaism with regards to marriage is the concept of intermarriage. This is when a Jew marries someone who is not Jewish, such as someone who belongs to another faith, or someone who is not religious at all. Some Jews, particularly older and Orthodox Jews, see intermarriage as an issue because it means that the new family is less likely to practice the Jewish faith. However, many younger and more liberal Jews are open to intermarriage.

Like Islam and Christianity, adultery is considered to be a sin in Judaism. This is because one of the Ten Commandments states "thou shalt not commit adultery."

Same-sex marriages are supported by many different Jewish groups. However, a Rabbi can choose not to perform same-sex weddings. In addition, Orthodox Jews tend to reject same-sex marriages since they reject same-sex relationships.

Divorce
Divorce is the act of ending a marriage, usually occurring when one or both members of a married couple deem that their marriage is no longer working for them. Divorce is a controversial area for all three of the faiths that we are discussing, since they all believe that marriage

is holy and an act of making a promise to one's spouse and to God. Divorce is seen as breaking that promise.

The Catholic Church is categorically opposed to divorce, and does not recognise divorces made by Catholics. However, the Catholic Church sometimes allows for annulments, in which a Priest deems a marriage 'nullified' because one or both of the members of the couple had no intention of keeping to their vows. For example, if one member of the couple did not want to have children, the marriage could be annulled as they were not keeping to the vow to have children. The Catholic Church believes that, since the vows were not upheld, the marriage never truly existed in the first place. This is different to a divorce, since divorces are the ending of a marriage.

Other Christian denominations, such as the Church of England, accept divorces. However, some churches might not accept remarriages of individuals who have been divorced in the past.

In Islam, divorce is also permitted. In Islam, a man may divorce his wife if he says "I divorce you" three times. Usually, there's a waiting period between each declaration, totalling to a nine-month waiting period. This exists to ensure that the wife is not pregnant. It is much harder for women to get a divorce in Islam – if it isn't written in their marriage contract, then a woman must go through the shari'ah courts. If the divorce is mutual, it is 'by khul'. If the divorce is not mutual, it is called a 'tafreeq divorce'. The husband and wife are allowed to re-marry after they have completed their divorce. Generally speaking, divorce is treated as a last resort, if the couple has exhausted all other ways to save their marriage.

A similar approach is taken in Judaism. Divorce is a last resort, only to be taken if all other routes have been unsuccessful. In Orthodox tradition, women cannot request the divorce – it must be the husband who initiates the process.

More liberal and progressive Jews accept divorce under more circumstances, and often allow for women to initiate the divorce.

Exam-Style Questions

Here are some questions you could be asked in your exam. The answers to these questions can be found in this chapter, so make sure you're able to answer all of them before moving on!

1. Explain why Christians believe that adultery is a sin. (4 marks)

2. Explain two similar religious views about marriage. (2 marks)

3. Explain two different religious beliefs about marriage. (2 marks)

4. Which religion allows for annulments of marriage, but not divorce? (1 mark)

5. "Religions should allow for divorce to happen, because it can make people happier than forcing them to stay in a marriage that they dislike." Evaluate this statement. (12 marks)

RELIGION, WAR, AND PEACE

War is an integral part of human history. If you look at a timeline of human history, there seems to have always been a war or other conflict happening. For this reason, Islam, Christianity, and Judaism all have teachings on war and peace. In this chapter, we'll be taking a look at:

- Religion and war;
- Religion and weapons of mass destruction.

Religion and War

Christianity, Islam, and Judaism are all religions which were founded during times of conflict. The early Christian Church was founded during Roman occupation and expansion throughout Europe and the Middle-East. Judaism developed during a time when many cultures and tribes fought against each other in the Middle-East. Islam was founded during a time of political turbulence in the 6th Century A.D. For this reason, war is an important part of these religions' histories and teachings. Let's find out what each religion's approach to war is.

Christianity and War

Jesus regularly taught against violence during his life. For example, he taught that we should 'turn the other cheek' when violence is done towards us. In addition, he regularly stated that we should love and forgive our enemies rather than resort to violence. Many Christians believe that Jesus was a pacifist, who approved of meekness and non-violence.

However, Jesus did show one sign of violence. When he discovered that the temple in Jerusalem had been filled with tradesmen, he cast them out by throwing tables and becoming indignant. For this reason, he wasn't completely devoid of violence. Some Christians use this as evidence that sometimes violence may be appropriate.

Many Christians are also pacifists, or support non-violence in the majority of cases. The Quakers, a Christian denomination, are completely opposed to violence and war. Individual cases of pacifism include Martin Luther King, a Civil Rights Activist who condemned violent action, instead using peaceful marches and rallies to help make lives better for black people in the USA during the 1960s. Dr King was a Baptist minister and a devout Christian.

While Jesus often taught against violence, Christianity is riddled

RELIGION, WAR, AND PEACE

with conflict. The 10th Century to 14th Century is filled with religious conflict as the Catholic Church organised crusades against Palestine in the Middle-East. Religion was often used as a justification for war. However, these conflicts are now considered to be a mistake, with many Christian denominations expressing shame regarding them.

Islam and War
The Qur'an teaches peace and kindness to all people. The Qur'an also teaches that to harm one person is to harm all of humanity. Therefore, Muslims should try not only to avoid violence, but also to actively prevent it in the world. With that said, the Qur'an does not teach outright pacifism, and therefore many Muslims believe that conflict can be justified in some circumstances.

Like Christianity, Islam has been involved in religious-motivated conflict. The crusades of the 11th, 12th, and 13th Century were mainly fought between Christians and Muslims, although it is often argued that since the Christians were the invaders and aggressors in the conflict, the Muslim combatants were not necessarily wrong to defend their land.

Judaism and War
Like Christianity and Islam, Judaism teaches that violence is to be avoided as much as possible. Peace is a gift from God, and therefore Jews should try to create as much peace in the world as possible.

Despite this, many Jews are not pacifists, and believe that there are wars that are justified. The concept of pikuach nefesh (preserve life) might involve killing someone who is dangerous, such as a terrorist, in order to save others. The Torah also states that killing in self-defence is acceptable if their own life is at risk, and that there were no other options left.

Judaism teaches a difference between obligatory war (milchemet mitzvah) and option war (milchemet reshut). Obligatory war is one which is commanded by God, or one that is necessary in order to defend one's homeland or innocent people. Optional war is usually considered to be immoral, since it concerns wars which were launched without exhausting other peace-keeping measures.

Just War
Just war is the idea that some war can be morally justified, making it

'just'. Different faiths have different attitudes towards just war.

Some, but not all, Christians support just war. These Christians believe that, in some cases, war is preferable to other consequences, such as genocide (mass murder of a race or nationality) or even more extreme conflict such as nuclear war. Some Christians believe that, in order to preserve peace, sometimes there has to be war. The Catholic Church's stance on war has changed over the years, but has generally supported just war.

Islam teaches that just war can exist. In Islam, this is known as a 'military jihad', with 'jihad' meaning 'struggle'. Some wars are considered to be condoned (allowed) by Allah so long as they protect Muslims and the Muslim faith. Sunni and Shi'a Muslims both support the idea of just war.

There are specific requirements which must be met before a war can be called a just war. These include wars which seek to end tyranny or liberate people, and in cases where Islamic countries have been invaded.

Judaism also supports just war. Pikuach nefesh, the preservation of life, can be used as justification for war if violence will help protect the lives of innocents. These would often be considered as obligatory wars.

Religion and Weapons of Mass Destruction (WMDs)

As the name suggests, 'weapons of mass destruction' refers to weaponry that is incredibly powerful, and capable of causing a significant amount of damage. Weapons of mass destruction is a term used to define the following types of weaponry:

1. Nuclear weapons, such as nuclear missiles and bombs (such as the nuclear bombs dropped on Hiroshima and Nagasaki in the Second World War). These weapons utilise atomic physics in order to create huge explosions, capable of levelling cities and destroying environments. These bombs also cause the areas hit to become irradiated, which inflicts further damage on the environment and human life.

2. Chemical and biological weapons, such as white phosphorus and

anthrax, which are capable of causing damage directly to humans.

Most countries are against the use of weapons of mass destruction in most cases. However, these weapons have been used in recent history.

Weapons of mass destruction are a more recent phenomenon, which means that the Bible, the Torah, and the Qur'an don't have teachings directly about them. However, religious teachings on war and violence can be used to also instruct on whether weapons of mass destruction should be used.

Many Christians believe that weapons of mass destruction, such as nuclear weapons, are immoral. This is because they are used to inflict death and suffering: something which Jesus specifically taught against throughout his ministry. However, some Christians believe that the threat of nuclear weapons is enough to keep some countries in check, preventing conflict.

Muslims tend to disagree with the possession and use of weapons of mass destruction, since they would kill innocent people if used. This attitude is even held by the leadership of Muslim countries, who sometimes condemn ownership of weapons of mass destruction and refuse to possess them.

Judaism has a number of teachings regarding the use of weapons of mass destruction. The Israeli Defence Forces are not to use weapons which cause mass damage to property or human beings, which means that they do not use weapons of mass destruction. In Deuteronomy 20, it is stated that women and children should be spared during conflict. This means that weapons of mass destruction, which kill indiscriminately, should not be used.

Exam-Style Questions

Here are some questions you could be asked in your exam. The answers to these questions can be found in this chapter, so make sure you're able to answer all of them before moving on!

1. Which of the major three religions has a doctrine on jihad? (1 mark)

2. Explain two religious beliefs about weapons of mass destruction. (2 marks)

3. Explain why some Christians are pacifists. (4 marks)

4. Explain the Jewish doctrine of pikuach nefesh. (4 marks)

5. "Religious people should never use violence." Evaluate this statement. (12 marks)

REVISION AND EXAM TIPS

Revision Timetables and Planning

Now that you've had the opportunity to explore the different ways of learning, it's time to turn the focus to other general aspects of revision: creating and sticking to a timetable, and making full use of revision materials. Both are extremely valuable when revising, and proper handling of both will improve your grade and make you more likely to score high in exams and in controlled assessments.

The goal of having a revision timetable is to map out all of the work that needs to be done in the time after you've started, up until your exams begin. Your plan doesn't need to be expertly crafted or even particularly nice to look at; it just needs to be clear and easy to read.

The first thing you should do is list every subject that you are taking exams in. Once you've done that, try and find every topic or module within that subject. For example, a breakdown of your history subject may look like this:

Module 1 – History of Medicine

- Diseases and infection: ancient era, renaissance era, industrial era, and modern era;
- Surgery and the human body: ancient surgery, medieval and renaissance surgery, and modern-day surgery;
- Public health: pre-industrial era, post-industrial era, and 20th century public health.

Module 2 – Elizabethan England

- Queen Elizabeth and her government;
- Treatment of the poor in Elizabethan England;
- Puritanism;
- Catholicism;
- Shakespeare and theatre in Elizabethan England;
- Naval expansion in Elizabethan England.

You may wish to go into slightly more detail for each of the topics, but as a foundation this will be enough to fill in a revision timetable. Do this for every module and for every subject so that you know roughly how much material there is to cover. It's also worth taking a look at how long each of the chapters for these modules are in your textbook, so that you're aware of any abnormally large or small topics.

Once you've done this, it's time to prioritise all of your subjects and topics. Some people like to rank all their subjects from most important to least important. In other words, it might be worth considering which subjects you find more difficult and giving them higher priority. If you already feel quite confident about a certain part of your studies, place it slightly lower on your list. This means that the areas that need the most attention will receive it.

Once you've prioritised your subjects, you can also prioritise modules. Bear in mind that a lot of topics in many subjects are cumulative – which means that a good understanding of earlier modules is vital for getting to grips with later ones. This is especially the case with maths and science, where you're building up knowledge as you go along. For these ones, it's better to start at the beginning and work your way through, but other subjects might allow you to mix things up a bit.

Your timetable should include all of the material you need to revise outside of school hours. The best way to find out what you need to cover is to take a look at how your textbooks divide their content, and then use those to fill the timetable. You'll be treated to some blank templates for a timetable at the end of this book. The following example timetable shows what a single week of revision during term-time may look like. Take a look at this timetable to get an idea of how to organise your time.

	Monday	Tuesday	Wednesday	Thursday	Friday	Saturday	Sunday
9:00am-10:00am	School	School	School	School	School	English - essay planning	Chemistry - mock paper
10:00am-11:00am	School	School	School	School	School	History - essay planning	Chemistry - mock paper
11:00am-12:00pm	School	School	School	School	School	English - mock essay	Physics - mock paper
12:00pm-1:00pm	School	School	School	School	School	History - mock essay	Physics - mock paper
1:00pm-2:00pm	School	School	School	School	School	Lunch break	Lunch break
2:00pm-3:00pm	School	School	School	School	School	Free time	Free time
3:00pm-4:00pm	School	School	School	School	School	Maths - mock paper	Biology - mock paper
4:00pm-5:00pm	Maths - algebra	Physics - electromagnets	Biology - human anatomy	Maths - statistics	History - The Spanish Armada	Mahts - mock paper	Biology - mock paper
5:00pm-6:00pm	Maths - trigonometry	Physics - space physics	Biology - homeostasis	English - spelling practice	History - Britain in WW2	Free time	Free time
6:00pm-7:00pm	Physics - forces	English - read 19th century novel	Maths - probability	English - anthology	English - anthology	Free time	Free time

Remember to factor in breaks and school time. During term time, you're going to be in school for most of the day, only giving you a couple of hours in the afternoon and evening. Naturally, you're going to feel more tired in the evenings after school than at the weekends, so you might find that doing the bulk of your revision on Saturday and Sunday is helpful, then doing much less during the week so that you don't feel completely swamped.

On the other hand, you might want to do all of your revision during the week, then have relatively little to do at the weekend. Spend the first two weeks of your revision trying out some different routines, find out what works best for you, then stick to one for the duration of the exam season.

During the school holidays, the game changes entirely. All of a sudden you don't have to go to school for 6 hours a day, meaning you have a lot more time on your hands. While you may want to take a break from everything, you should make use of all the free time you have during these breaks. In fact, many students do the bulk of their revision during these holidays. Of course, you should take some time off, but make sure you take advantage of the holiday period. It can really put you ahead for the next term.

How do I motivate myself?

Getting motivated to revise in the first place can be incredibly difficult, and requires a lot of determination and self-control. The earlier you start your revision, the better, but you'll probably be tempted to put off revision: "I'll start next week", or "it's way too early to start revising." Try and start revising 8 weeks before your first exam. This should give you plenty of time to get through all of your topics.

However, even starting the process can be a pain, and when the exams are so far away it's difficult to get the ball rolling. So, you need to motivate yourself to start revising as early and as well as possible. Here are some ways to inspire yourself to start revising.

Revision Styles
Start by finding revision styles that you actually enjoy. This might sound ridiculous, but if you can find a few techniques that aren't completely unbearable, you'll be more willing to make a start with revision. Remember that you don't have to be constantly doing 'hard revision'

such as note-taking. Mix things up and try a number of styles to keep things fresh early on, then maybe move into something more serious later.

Ease into it
Before you start, revision can feel like a huge mountain, impossible to climb to the top of. It can be incredibly daunting. You might be overwhelmed by the feeling that you are completely unprepared and don't know enough. That said, you need to make a start sometime. Some revision is better than no revision at all, so if you're struggling to get started with your studies, ease your way into it. Start by revising for a much shorter period of time, and maybe focus on the things that you already know well or most enjoy. Once you're comfortable and confident, move onto something that you're less sure of.

Treat Yourself
Make sure to keep yourself motivated with some treats. You don't need to go overboard, but the "carrot and stick" method of revision can keep you working for longer periods of time, allowing you to get through more work. Things like "I'll get some ice cream, but only after I've done the next 3 pages" are a great way of keeping you going and keeping your spirits up.

Think Ahead
Finally, always think ahead past exams. Life continues after your GCSEs, and you'll be treated to an extra-long summer once you've finished. You might feel that you're not in a great place while revising, that your social life is suffering or your free time is being eaten up by studies, but it will all be worth it when you get great results. This positive outlook – thinking towards the future – is one of the best ways to get you started with revision, and keep you going with it too.

Staying Focused
Sometimes, revision can be a total pain, and you'd rather do anything (even sit around doing absolutely nothing!) than open a book and do some hard learning. It's very tempting to procrastinate, but falling into the trap of putting off revision is one of the biggest mistakes you can possibly do. Here are our top 5 tips for avoiding procrastination and getting on with your work!

1. Turn off distractions

The first thing you should do before starting a revision session is remove any distractions from your workspace. The biggest offenders of distracting pupils are games consoles, social media, mobile phones, and of course television. The simple solution to this is to turn off these devices and put them somewhere out of view or reach, so you aren't tempted to turn them back on and continue texting, messaging or playing games.

Sometimes, however, it isn't practical to move all of these devices. In this case, it's better to find a new workspace, free of electronic devices and other distractions. Many people find that their kitchen or dining room table is an excellent place to study, but find what works best for you and your home. If there's nowhere in your house that's suitable for studying, the local library may be a good choice.

When choosing a place to study, consider the following:

- Is it quiet?
- Are there any gadgets to distract you?
- Will people be walking in and out of the room? Will that distract you?
- Is it comfortable?
- Is there plenty of room for you and all of your notes?

Things get a little trickier when you're using computerised or other online resources such as revision games or podcasts. In these cases, you're going to need your computer, phone or tablet with you, so you'll need to exercise some self-control. Log yourself out of social media if you feel that it's necessary to do so, and make sure to turn off notifications for messaging apps on your phone. You can always take a look during your breaks.

Finally, a few words about listening to music while revising. Be very careful when playing music (especially music with lyrics) while studying. It works for some people, but others will find it incredibly distracting. Experiment with it for yourself, but if you find it doesn't help you, promptly turn it off.

> **Advice for Parents**
>
> *If possible, make sure that your child has a dedicated space to revise in. Preferably, this place should be far away from any kind of distraction, including noise caused by family. Try to keep the noise down while your child is revising, but occasionally popping in to show support can make a world of difference.*

2. Give yourself plenty of breaks (but not too many!)

Believe it or not, one of the best ways to avoid procrastination is to take regular breaks. Concentration tends to slide after 45 minutes for a lot of teenagers, so don't push yourself to revise for longer periods of time. If you do this, you'll likely get distracted by almost everything around you, or just get bored or tired. The solution to this problem is to place regular breaks after every chunk of time spent revising. So, if you revise for 45 minutes, you should give yourself a 10 or 15-minute break afterwards. Start with this and then adjust it as necessary until you get a routine which is comfortable for you.

Remember not to go overboard with breaks, though! Make sure that you stick to your timetable and routine, so that a 15-minute break doesn't turn into an hour spent watching TV!

3. Stick to your revision timetable

Writing and filling in a revision timetable is one thing, but it's another thing entirely to stick to it throughout your entire exam season. If it helps, make your timetable more detailed to include breaks and other activities.

It can be tempting to put off revision or bargain with yourself: "I'll only do 2 hours today but I'll make up for it tomorrow," or "I don't really need to know this stuff, I'll take the rest of the day off." Both of these are risky mindsets which don't put you in a great place for succeeding. Good organisation skills come in handy here, and you should try and keep to your timetable as much as possible.

Of course, you can be flexible with your time. Sometimes things come up, and you shouldn't completely sacrifice your social life during the revision period. Just make sure it's reasonable, though.

4. Make your working environment comfortable

Outside of keeping things quiet and free from distracting gadgets, you should make sure that your revision space is comfortable enough for you to work in. If the room is too cold or hot, or your chair isn't comfortable to sit on, then you might find yourself not wanting to revise. Make sure your revision space is as comfortable as possible.

> **Advice for Parents**
>
> *Ask your child if they like their revision space. If they don't, find out what the problem is and try to help them solve it.*

5. Mix things up

The final tip for staying focused is to mix things up every so often. One way to do this is to change the subject that you're revising halfway through the day. This means that you'll still be revising and you'll keep things fresh. You don't need to switch it up too often, but when you find yourself getting too bored of a topic to continue, finish it and then move onto something else entirely, preferably an area from another subject.

You could also change your revision techniques from time to time to keep things interesting. If you've spent the whole morning writing notes, why not switch over to a podcast or some learning games? You can refer back to our section on different learning styles to get some ideas on how you can make your revision more varied.

Avoid Cramming!

Cramming is the act of trying to stuff in as much revision as possible in the days (or even hours!) just before the exam. It's also possibly the biggest act of sabotage that you can do to yourself.

Cramming happens when a pupil either does very little or no revision before the exams. Before they know it, the exam dates have crept up on them, sending them into a state of panic. These pupils tend to then rush through their textbooks and materials, trying to cover weeks' worth of work in just a few days. In almost every case, this is simply not enough time to adequately revise everything. So, people who cram very rarely benefit from it.

Cramming can actually worsen your performance in an exam. Students who cram often find themselves completely blanking on information when they start answering questions, leaving them helpless during an exam. Cramming doesn't work because you aren't giving your brain enough time to let information sink in.

In an ideal world, you should try to finish your revision for a subject 2 or 3 days before the exam starts. This doesn't always go to plan, but aim to have your revision finished at least 2 days before. Revising the night before an exam is a bad idea, and you should avoid doing so. The day before your exam (and in the hours leading up to it as well) should be spent relaxing and keeping calm, eating well and not allowing yourself to become stressed out by looming thoughts about the test. If you get to the day before your exam and you've finished everything, then you've done an excellent job, and deserve an evening to relax.

Advice for Parents

Keep an eye on your child's revision schedule, and every so often check that they're on top of their work. You don't want to intrude too much, but a subtle reminder might make sure that your child doesn't let their exams creep up on them.

Conclusion

So, by this point you hopefully have the following: a revision timetable, a comfortable space to work, an idea of what your learning style is, and some ideas to get you started with revision. You're well on your way to taking on your GCSEs and succeeding.

Next, we'll be looking at exams: what they are, how to deal with revising for them and how to perform well in them!

EXAM TECHNIQUES AND PREPARATION

What are Exams?

So, now you hopefully have your exam timetable ready, with some learning and revision techniques to get you on your way.

At some point during your GCSEs, you're going to come across at least one exam. This is pretty much unavoidable because every subject at GCSE uses examinations to assess your knowledge, understanding and ability. Exams can be incredibly taunting, but in this chapter you'll learn what they are and how to deal with them effectively.

An exam is a type of test that you take in a controlled environment. In most cases, exams test your knowledge and understanding. You will need to remember information that you've learned for the subject throughout your GCSE years. Sometimes you'll just need to recall facts, but in other cases you'll have to apply your understanding and knowledge to a situation. This could involve essay writing (such as in English or history), or problem solving (such as in maths).

This means that you have to sit in silence, for at least 45 minutes (and often longer), and finish a paper full of questions. The length of the exam will differ depending on the subject, module, and even exam board. If you are unsure about the length of any of your exams, speak to your teacher or check the relevant exam board websites.

Exam conditions are incredibly strict. Once you enter the exam hall, you can't speak to anyone. You are strictly limited to the time given to the exam, and if you're caught cheating in any way, you can be disqualified from all of your exams.

Thankfully, it isn't all doom and gloom. Exams are tough, but they aren't designed to be impossible or even cruel. If you prepare effectively using the tips and techniques in this book, and revise lots, you'll be more than ready to take on your exams.

Advice for Parents

If your child is unsure about what exams they are sitting, give them a hand by finding out what exam boards they are on. Once you've done this, head to the exam board's site(s) to find out details on the exams that your child is going to sit.

Types of Exam

There are a number of different kinds of exam you might sit. Here are some of the most common kinds:

- **Essay exams.** These exams require you to write longer pieces of work rather than answer lots of small questions. These will be most common in English literature and English language.

- **Short-question exams.** These exams will have lots of questions, each being worth a smaller amount of marks than a full question in an essay exam. Marks usually vary in length depending on how much the question is asking from you. Single-world answers are usually only worth one mark, whilst a longer maths question might be worth 3, 5 or even 10 marks. Short exam questions will show up across

- **Hybrid exams.** These exams will feature longer and shorter questions, as well as some essay questions. History and science exams often have slightly longer essays as well as some shorter questions at GCSE.

As well as this, there are some further general exams that you might have to sit:

- **Listening exams.** This is most common in modern foreign languages. You'll have a recording played to you, and you will need to answer questions in a booklet based on what you are hearing.

- **Speaking exams.** Again, these are quite common when studying a foreign language. Unlike your other exams, speaking exams usually won't require you to enter an exam hall with lots of other students. Instead, you'll sit one to one with a member of staff and will have to speak to them in a language. They will ask questions, and you'll have to answer back in the language that you're studying.

The Tiers: Foundation and Higher

Currently, GCSEs are split into two tiers – foundation and higher. Depending on your ability, you will be entered in to your GCSEs at one of these two levels. There are a few differences between the two tiers that you need to know about, since they affect what type of exam you will sit.

Firstly, the content of a course may differ depending on whether you're on the foundation or higher tier. Some subjects are quite similar in structure between the two tiers, but may offer different content. For example, a foundation-tier maths course may contain the same format and kind of questions as a higher-tier course, but students in the higher-tier will be expected to have a better understanding of maths, and also be able to complete more demanding questions.

In other subjects, the mark scheme will be different depending on the tier students sit. For example, a foundation-tier English paper might ask students to describe a scene from a book that they've studied, whilst a higher-tier exam may ask for analysis or evaluation as well. For this reason, it's important to know what tier you're being entered for before starting revision, attempting mock papers or reading mark schemes.

As we've established, higher-tier papers are generally more demanding than foundation-tier exams. They'll either contain trickier content, expect a higher level of analysis or discussion, or have a different structure. Quite often, a higher-tier exam will consist of all three of these differences.

So, why take a higher-tier course if it's generally harder? The benefit of sitting a higher-tier paper is that you will be able to get a higher grade. Students on a foundation-tier course can get a grade between 1 and 5, whilst the grading for higher-tier courses ranges from the middle of a level 3 up to a level 9.

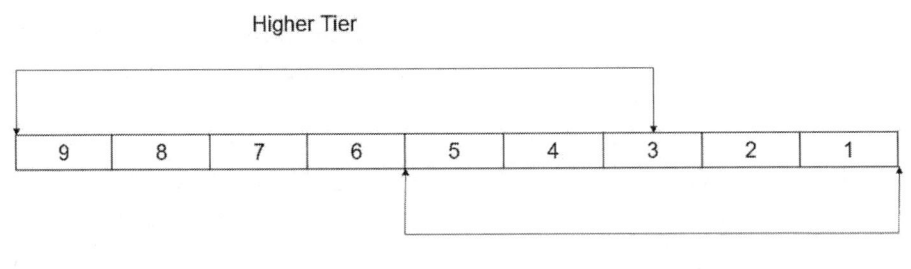

Higher Tier

| 9 | 8 | 7 | 6 | 5 | 4 | 3 | 2 | 1 |

Foundation Tier

It's in your best interest to find out what tier you're going to be on. Remember that tiers can differ between subjects, so don't assume you're in one tier for every one of your GCSEs. Ask your teachers what tier you're going to be entered for so that you know what to prepare for in the exams.

Exam Tips and Techniques

Exams can be difficult, and you need to prepare for them in two different ways. First, you need to know the content of the exam. This is the actual information you are going to be tested on – the stuff you've been learning in lessons.

The second thing you need to learn is how to answer exam questions, and how to perform well in exams. This might sound strange, but a significant part of doing well in exams comes down to your familiarity with them, not just how well you know your subjects.

In a later chapter, we'll discuss subject-specific tips for exams. For now, take a look at these general tips which will help you in the days before and during your exams.

Come Prepared

Always make sure that you have all of the equipment necessary for completing an exam. This will depend on the subject and the module, so find out beforehand what you're allowed to take in with you.

The following are things you can take into almost any exam:

- **Black pens.** You should always take a few black, ballpoint pens into your exams. Generally speaking, blue pens are not allowed, neither are fountain-pen designs, since the ink can run more easily on them. Ballpoints are the standard for most exam boards.

- **Pencils.** You might not need these for every exam, but it's worth bringing them for rough planning, just in case.

- **Clear pencil case.** Again, this might not be necessary, but bringing a pencil case can help you be more organised. Make sure it's clear, though – if the exam invigilators can't see into the pencil case easily, they may confiscate it because you could be using it to hide notes and cheat!

- **Bottle of water.** We'll talk more about this later on, but bringing a bottle of water can help you concentrate – you don't want to get dehydrated. Remember to make sure that the bottle is clear and has no labels.

Depending on the exam, other pieces of equipment may be appropriate, such as:

- **Calculator.** Certain maths and science exams will allow you to bring calculators. Other exams in these subjects might not allow for calculators. If you aren't sure, bring it with you anyway and then leave it under your desk, and hand it to an invigilator if it isn't allowed.

- **Rulers and protractors.** Equipment for solving angles may be allowed for some exams. Like calculators, however, they won't be allowed for others. Make sure that they are transparent (clear).

- **Books.** Be careful with this one. Some exams might allow you to bring in a specific book, such as some English or language exams. Others will be referred to as 'closed-book' exams, which means you can't take in any notes or materials – including the books that you've studied.

If you aren't sure which equipment you're allowed to bring into the exam, ask your teacher well in advance.

Keep Calm

Getting a handle on your nerves can be really difficult during exam season, but remember that this is completely normal. If you consider that doing well in your GCSEs is very important, then it would be bizarre for you not to be at least a bit nervous. Millions of people will be going through the same thing as you, and millions more have been in your position and have made it out of the other end in one piece. Life goes on after your GCSEs, even if it doesn't feel like that during the heat of an exam.

Exams are stressful, and the conditions you take them in aren't pleasant either. Being stuck in a silent room for an hour, with nothing but a question paper and your own thoughts, can be incredibly daunting. However, you need to remember that you're not the only one who feels this way, and that a bit of nerves can give you the boost you need in the exam hall.

That said, you need to keep any anxiety under control. A breakdown just before the exam (or even worse, during it) is uncommon, but just remember that not doing as well as you'd hoped in a single exam isn't the end of the world.

You might feel as though you aren't prepared enough, or perhaps a classmate has made you unsure about what you've revised – minutes before entering the exam room. This happens often, and be incredibly demoralising. Remember that how prepared you think you are doesn't necessarily represent how well prepared you actually are. Sometimes, people who feel poorly prepared for some exams in the minutes before taking it end up doing incredibly well, and sometimes find themselves doing worse in exams they felt completely ready for. Some people find themselves taking it easy and getting a bit too comfortable in some exams because they think they know it all, but someone who feels a little unsure goes in and gives it their all, and ends up doing much better. Essentially, you never truly know how prepared you are.

Besides, what's the use in worrying on the day of the exam? There's no time left to go back and revise some more, so there's no point in getting stressed about it once you're in the room. Try and get into the current moment and power through it.

Here are some other tips for keeping calm in the exam:

- **Breathing exercises.** If you find yourself getting nervous before exams, or struggle to get to sleep due to exam anxiety, then breathing exercises could be beneficial.

- **Get into the moment.** Just before and during your exam, it can help to go into "exam-mode". By this, we mean blocking off outside distractions and any negativity coming from anywhere. Sometimes, having friends and classmates talk about the possible contents of the exam just before entering can put you off. It might make you feel as if you've missed out on something major, and then cause you to worry once you enter the exam room. Put all of this out of your mind as soon as you enter the room. Once you're in the exam, there's no use fretting about those details.

- **Positive thinking**. This might seem obvious, but thinking positively about the exam and what comes after can be extremely helpful. Some people like to change their mindset about exams, thinking of it as an opportunity to show off their knowledge rather than a painful task that they have to work their way through. Alternatively, focus on what you **do** know rather than what you **don't** know, what you **can** do rather than what you **can't** do. Once you're in the exam room, there's no point worrying about your weaknesses. Focus on your strengths.

Read Instructions Carefully

This sounds simple, but far too many people trip up on this simple bit of advice. When you enter your exam, the first thing you should do is read the instructions on the front of the question or answer paper. In some cases, an invigilator may read the instructions to you, but feel free to read the instructions before the exam starts.

Keep an eye out for instructions on what questions to answer. In some exams, you'll have a choice of which questions you answer, rather than having to answer every question. In these cases, you need to make sure that you know exactly what's required of you, so that you don't waste time answering questions that you don't need to answer. The only thing worse than finding out at the end of the exam that you answered questions unnecessarily is realising that you didn't answer enough of them!

When you are given a choice of two or more questions to answer (especially in essay subjects), make sure you clearly show which questions you are answering. In some exams, you'll have to tick a box to show what question you're attempting, whilst others will require you to write the question number in your answer section. Either way, keep an eye on the instructions before going ahead and starting the question. This will prevent you from wasting time answering questions that you don't need to attempt, and also stop you from accidentally missing questions that need answering.

When it comes to some questions, more things may be required from you than just giving a single answer. In a lot of maths exams, you will be asked to show your working. By this, it's simply meant that you must show how you got to your answer if you want to get more marks. Sometimes, minimal marks are given if you don't show your working, so it's vital that you include how you made your way to the answer. Keep an eye out for questions which specify that you must "show your working" – you'll need to make sure that you do it to get as many marks as possible.

Answer the Easiest Questions First

This tip is absolutely key for the tougher exams you come across, since it's an excellent way to use your time in the exam hall effectively.

Say you're about to sit an exam. You sit down and have the examination instructions read out to you. The invigilator informs you to start your exam, and then you begin. You open the question booklet to find that the first question seems almost impossible. Before you panic, take a flick through the booklet and take a look at some of the other questions. If possible, pick the question that looks the easiest to you and start with that.

This is a good technique for two reasons. Firstly, it's a great boost to your confidence when you're feeling unsure about the exam. There's not much worse in an exam than sitting there, becoming more and more demoralised by a question that you don't think you can answer. Starting with more manageable questions will help you ease into the exam, and hopefully you'll recall some information while doing it.

Sometimes, exams can fit together like a puzzle. At first, it seems impossible. But, once you start to put pieces in (answer the questions), the more difficult bits start to make sense. All of a sudden, you're on a roll of answering questions, and then the tough ones don't seem so bad!

The other reason that this is a good technique is that it is an effective use of your time. There's no point sitting and staring blankly at a question you can't solve when there are others that you could be getting on with. Forget about the tough questions for now, bank as many marks you can get with the easier ones, then go back to them at the end if you have time. This way, you can secure as many marks as possible. In the worst-case scenario, you won't be able to complete the tough questions, but you'll still have earned a few points for all of the others.

Answer the Question
One of the biggest mistakes that students make throughout their academic lives is failing to answer the question that they've been asked. This is particularly the case for essay-based exams such as English literature, but applies to all of your exams.

Focus on Key Details
Some students have a tendency of reading a question briefly, then jumping straight into their answer without thinking about what's really being asked. For questions which are worth lots of marks, you should take extra care in reading the question fully. If it helps, underline the key parts of the question so that it's easier to break down:

> What were the main causes of the First World War?

This becomes:

> What were the main causes of the First World War?

We can figure out a few things from underlining the key points in this question. Firstly, we know that the topic of the question is the First World War. In particular, we need to be looking at the causes of the war. So, our answer is going to be focused on the time period leading up to the start of the First World War in 1914.

However, there's more to the question than this. This question specifies the "main" causes of the First World War. So, we don't need to talk about every single cause of the war, just a few of the most important or biggest things which caused the First World War to happen, such as the assassination of Archduke Franz Ferdinand and rising tensions between the European empires.

Already, we've figured out that we need to answer the question in the following way:

- You need to talk about the causes of the First World War (events up to 1914).
- You need to limit your answer to the main (biggest) causes of the war.

Highlighting the key points of the question has proven useful because it's pointed out exactly what the question is asking of us. This means that we can save time by answering exactly what we need to, rather than talking about things that won't get us any extra marks.

Don't Twist the Question

Sometimes, students see a question that they don't particularly like the look of. Perhaps it's for a topic that they've studied well and enjoyed, but the question takes it in a slightly different direction to one that they're used to. For example, a student may have studied the Shakespeare play *Othello* as part of English literature, and really liked the dastardly villain, Iago. In the exam, they might come across a question on the play, but not specifically about Iago. The question could be:

> How does Shakespeare show the relationship between Othello and his wife, Desdemona?

This question is primarily focused on the main character, Othello, and his wife, Desdemona. While the character of Iago plays into most elements of *Othello*, it might be tricky to include him in a discussion about the relationship between Othello and Desdemona. So, you'd need to avoid straying from the topic of the question, even if there's something you would rather write about. Twisting the question into something that you want to answer is a trap that quite a lot of students fall into, and this ends up costing them marks – particularly in essay subjects. Writing a short plan for your answer, and reading the question carefully, can help you avoid this.

Double-Check the Question

In the next section, we'll be talking about double-checking answers, but it's just as important to double-check the question that you're answering before you begin to answer it. Say you're doing a maths question:

$$8.93 \times 9.54 = ?$$

Before you start answering the question, take note of everything about it. Where are the decimal points? What operation needs to be performed? Sometimes, people make silly mistakes and misread the question, getting things mixed up.

It's not pleasant finding out that you've answered a question incorrectly just as you get to the end of it, so it pays to look over the question multiple times. In the case of maths questions, it might help to re-write the question in the answer box if there's space. This means you can look back at it quickly, without making any mistakes.

Don't Hedge Your Bets

Hedging your bets happens when a student tries to give 2 or more answers to a single question, trying to cover as many bases as possible and be less likely to lose marks. After all, if you give lots of different answers, surely one of them is bound to be correct? The problem with this is that examiners will mark harshly against answers like these. Take a look at this example of someone who has tried to hedge their bets:

Question: What part of the human body carries blood back to the heart?

Answer: Veins/Arteries

Only one of the given answers can be correct, since one of them sends blood away from the heart and the other brings blood back to it. The correct answer is "veins", but in this example, both possible answers have been put in. This example answer shows that whoever answered the question wasn't sure, so put both down just in case. Examiners will not award marks for this, so it's essential that you don't try to play it safe in this way. Be confident in your answer.

Avoid Blanking

Have you ever been in a situation where you had something in your head that you were about to say, or about to write, but then completely forgot what it was just before saying or writing it? It can be frustrating it everyday life, but when it happens in an exam it can lead to all kinds of problems. Key details can be forgotten, formulas and tricks may be hard to recall and sometimes you might just struggle to get off the first page. This is what people refer to as 'blanking'.

Blanking is something that many students worry about, and you've likely heard some horror stories about people who have forgotten everything just as they enter the exam room. However, it doesn't occur as often as you might think, and it doesn't mean you're going to fail your exam.

The best way to prevent blanking is to keep stress to a minimum. This might be easier said than done, but students tend to blank when they haven't had much sleep or have tried to cram their revision into the day before, or the day of the exam itself. This can cause students to panic, and while they're busy worrying, anything that might have been holding in their short-term memory gets forgotten. We'll cover stress in more detail later in this chapter.

In addition to keeping stress to a minimum, make sure that you aren't revising on the day of your exam, and preferably not the night before, either. In order to retain the information in your revision, you need to commit it to what some people call your 'long-term memory'. It takes time for what you've studied to reach this part of your memory, and things revised in the hours before the exam usually haven't made it there. When revision is being held in the short-term memory, you're generally more likely to forget it, which in turn leads to blanking.

If you find that you've blanked in your exam, here are some tips to keep you calm and help you recover from it as quickly as possible:

Take a few deep breaths before continuing. This is important as you need to stay calm. The more you panic, the less likely you are to remember the information you need. Take a moment to calm down – remember that not performing so well on this exam isn't the end of the world, and that you have the entire paper to remember what you need to know and get back on form.

Look through the question booklet. Sometimes, the wording of a question can jog your memory, or give you a clue of what to write. This can get you started on an answer, which in turn can set off a chain-reaction of memories flooding back, to the point where you remember plenty of information. However, this doesn't always happen; don't rely on this as a replacement for revising over a longer period of time.

Start with an easier question. Some questions require less knowledge than others. If you find yourself blanking in the exam, go onto a question that doesn't need as much precise information as others. Sometimes, a question won't be asking for specific terms or details, but rather an analysis or critical take on the material. These are the questions to do first if you find yourself blanking. This won't work for every kind of exam, however.

Don't attempt any of the larger questions. It might be tempting to just throw caution to the wind and get the toughest or biggest question out of the way. This is usually a bad idea, since these questions contain the most marks. You want to answer these once you've remembered as much as possible, so wait until later in the exam to try them.

It's not the end of the world. If you find yourself running out of time, don't panic. Answer as many questions as you can to secure as many marks as possible. It isn't the end of the world if you don't do so well, and you'll have other exams to pick up some marks in.

Double-Check Your Work
Everyone makes mistakes. It's almost completely unavoidable, even under relaxed conditions, to create a piece of work that's free of any errors at all. In an exam, you're going to feel a bit rushed, and you're probably going to be working very quickly. This is fine, but remember that you're more likely to make mistakes this way. So, it's important that you go back and check everything you've written. Small, silly errors can cost you big marks, so it's vital that you make sure you've

fixed anything that could be wrong.

Proofreading can take place at two times during your exam. You can either re-read each of your answers individually after you've completed each one, or you can go back at the end of the exam (if you have time) and check everyone in one go. There are benefits and drawbacks to both:

Proofread as you go

Pros	Cons
You're more likely to have time to double-check your answers	If you spend too long proofreading, you might not finish the exam
You can take the exam bit by bit	You might be in "exam-mode" and not as relaxed as at the end of the exam

Proofread at the end

Pros	Cons
You can focus on finishing the exam first before going back to check	If you take too long doing the exam, you might not have time to proofread towards the end
You'll probably be more relaxed once you've answered all the questions	

Both have pros and cons, and one method may just suit you better. You might prefer the methodical approach of checking every answer once you've finished it. Alternatively, you might find it easier to handle the exam, know that you've answered every question that you can, and then go back and check everything in one go.

How to go about proofreading your work will depend on the subject that you're taking, and the questions that you've been asked. If you've had to write essays or other longer bits of text, read over your work, checking for errors. Re-read the question, and make sure that you've answered how it wants you to. If you haven't done this, quickly add the extra information in the answer box.

If you've missed something out of an essay, the best thing to do is put a little asterisk symbol (*) where you'd like to add more information. Then, in the next available space (possible even at the end of the essay), put another asterisk, followed by the information that you've missed out on.

When you double-check your work, you might come across something that you've written, but you also know now that it's incorrect. In this case, you need to cross it out so the person marking your exam knows to ignore these incorrect parts. Put a straight, diagonal line through your work to indicate any work that you don't want the examiner to look at. Then, all you need to do is replace what you've crossed out with something that's correct.

Bring Some Water and Eat Healthily
You are allowed to bring a bottle of water into almost any exam. There may be a couple of exceptions for practical-based exams such as art, but aside from that, water is allowed. In fact, bringing a bottle of water to drink in an exam is largely encouraged, because it can help you relax and concentrate.

Some studies show that students who take a bottle of water into their exams and drink it get an average score of 5% higher than students who do not. While this might not actually happen for you, it suggests that having a bottle of water handy can be helpful.

On the same topic, eating healthily (and sensibly!) before your exams can make a substantial difference. Try and avoid drinking sugary, fizzy drinks or sweets before an exam. The sugar rush might make you feel on top of the world when the exam starts, but you could have a crash halfway through, leaving you shattered for the final stretch. Instead, try and have a good breakfast in the morning before your exams. See what works best for you, but eggs and fish (such as smoked salmon) can give you plenty of energy to complete your exams with.

In addition to this, some exams may allow you to bring in a small piece of food to eat. Fruit is always a safe bet, including bananas and apples. Basically, you want something that doesn't take too long to eat, but gives you enough of a boost to help you through the exam. Remember to check that you're allowed to take food into your exam before doing so.

Stay Healthy

No matter what happens in your exams, it's important that you stay healthy. This is a slightly more general point, but it can't be emphasised enough.

First, you need to stay mentally healthy. Remember that there's life after your exams, and so you shouldn't put yourself under unnecessary pressure. Some anxiety is unavoidable, but it's important that you don't let it get out of control. Between exams, remember to do things that you enjoy, be it sports, video-games, reading fiction, watching television or spending time with friends or family. This will help you feel calm during your exam period, and remind you that there's more to life than your GCSEs!

Secondly, you need to think about your physical wellbeing. While you're busy revising and making yourself ready to ace the exams, it's easy to forget about your own health. While it's good to take revision seriously, you can't neglect your own physical needs, and so you should make sure to get a lot of the following during your exam period:

- **Sleep.** Everyone needs sleep in order to function, and you're no different! Teenagers need between 8 and 10 hours of sleep per night, so you should be aiming for this as well. A good night's sleep, particularly the night before your exam, can make a world of difference on the day of the test. It will also help you massively during your revision time.

- **A balanced diet.** This can be easily overlooked, but being fed well can be the key to acing an exam on the day. You want to feel as prepared as possible, so be sure to get a satisfying meal the night before and on the day of your exam. Also try to eat plenty of fruit and vegetables, since they help strengthen your immune system. Some students work themselves extremely hard, then forget to boost their immunity to colds and flu by eating well. You want to avoid this – being ill during an exam is horrible!

Planning and Timing Your Exam

Good planning and timing are two of the most important skills that you can learn and practice before sitting your exams. In fact, being able to plan effectively and get your timings down will serve you well in almost every career, so it pays to put the effort in now.

Before you go into your exam, you should find out exactly what the structure of the exam will be. Try and find out the answers to the following questions:

- How long do I have for the whole exam?
- What type of questions will be asked (essay, single-word answer, short paragraph, problem solving, mathematical sums)?
- How many marks are there in the whole exam?
- Roughly, how many marks are available per question?
- If applicable, how much time is there for planning?

Once you have this information, you can get to work on applying this to your revision schedule. For example, when you attempt a mock exam, you should try to make the situation as close to the real thing as possible. You should plan and time your mock exam as if it were an actual exam. You can find more about planning and timing your exams in the chapter on subject-specific advice.

Using Mock Exams and Practice Questions

Once you're well into your revision, you'll find that you've got lots of information swimming around in your head. When you feel like you're getting to this point, it may be time to attempt a mock exam. These are excellent ways of testing how much you already know, and it also gives you an insight into what you still need to do in order to ace your exams.

Mock exams are so useful that some people use them and no other techniques when revising. This isn't strictly advised – it's better that you start by revising your notes before trying a mock test, mainly because you may not know enough or remember enough to fully complete a mock exam.

How do I find mock exams?
Finding mock exams is usually quite easy. The first port of call is your school or your teacher. It's possible that they have some mock exams already printed to give to you. If they don't, then it might be worth suggesting that they make some available for yourself and other students.

If your teacher doesn't have any mock exams prepared, try and find out as much about the exam(s) you want to revise for before looking up papers. The easiest resources to access are past papers, or actual exams from previous years. These are free to download from exam board websites and can be read from your computer screen, or printed off so that you can write on them.

In addition, there are plenty of workbooks specific to your subjects which will include practice papers and sample questions. You can find out about our range of GCSE workbooks at the end of this book, or navigate to https.//www.How2Become.com/education/.

Advice for Parents

Printing pages upon pages of past papers can get expensive, but it can be a vital way for your child to learn where their strengths lie and where they need to improve. A solution which will allow your child to take advantage of mock papers as well as save you money on printer ink is to find settings on your printer such as 'draft' or 'ink saver' mode. These will print the past papers out in a slightly lower quality, but usually the papers are still entirely useable.

How should I use mock exams?
There are two different ways to use mock exams in your revision. The first way is to attempt a full mock essay as you work through topics of the subject. For example, say that you have a science exam with three different sections. One of these sections is on evolution and adaptation, the next is on the human anatomy, and the concluding section is about how drugs and other substances can have an effect on the body. You figure out that these are the three topics you need to learn, so you go through past papers online, focusing on questions revolving around these three topics.

Alternatively, you can work through every topic for the exam, and then move onto past papers. The advantage of this method means that you can spend a chunk of time focusing completely on taking notes and using other revision techniques, then move onto working through whole mock papers. This means that you can simulate the experience of being in an actual exam.

Simulating exam conditions
Mock papers and past papers are really useful because they allow you

to sit a test as if it was the real thing. To do this, find out how much time you would be given to finish the paper in an actual exam – this information can usually be found on the front of the past paper. Then, gather your pens, pencils and other tools, put your notes aside and find a quiet place. Then, get to work with the mock test.

Time yourself with a clock or stopwatch (most mobile phones come equipped with a stopwatch), and see how long it takes you to complete the paper. What's even more useful is to time how long each section, or even each question, takes you to complete. So, if you find yourself running short on time, you know exactly which topics or types of question need greater focus. You don't want to try and speed through your paper too quickly, but if you're taking an unusually long amount of time on shorter questions, then you know that you need to improve on them.

The best part of using mock exams and past papers is that you can put yourself to the test, and make sure of two things. Firstly, you can make sure that you can recall the material you'll need to remember in the real exam. This comes into effect when you simulate a real exam environment, by doing the test under timed conditions and without your notes. While you're doing the mock tests, you'll probably get an idea of what you can and can't recall. Whenever you can't remember the answer to a question, or there's a key fact you can't recall, make a note on a spare sheet of paper, or at the side of your answer booklet. Then, once you finish the paper, you know exactly what you need to go back to and revise some more.

Mock tests are also useful because they highlight things that you thought you knew, but perhaps didn't get entirely correct. This will become clear when you take a look at the mark scheme, which we will cover in more detail later on in this chapter.

After the past papers...
Once you're finished with the mock paper, look at the mark scheme and see how well you did. For subjects with clear "right or wrong" answers, such as maths or science, this is quite easy – all you need to do is read the answer then see if it matches what you wrote. For essay-based subjects such as English, this is trickier since the answers you give aren't necessarily right or wrong. In these exams, you tend to be judged on how well you write rather than what you write exactly. In this case, you might need help from your teacher.

Ask your teacher to take a look at your past papers, and they might be able to take a quick look at it. If they have the time, they might go ahead and mark it properly, giving you an idea of where you've done well and where you need to improve. If possible, get a full breakdown of marks so you know exactly what aspects of your exam you need to focus on.

In the next section, we'll examine at mark schemes in more detail. You'll learn how they work, and more importantly how to use them in to make your revision more focused. For now, feast your eyes on the flowcharts on the next page. These show two different ways of including mock tests in your revision strategy.

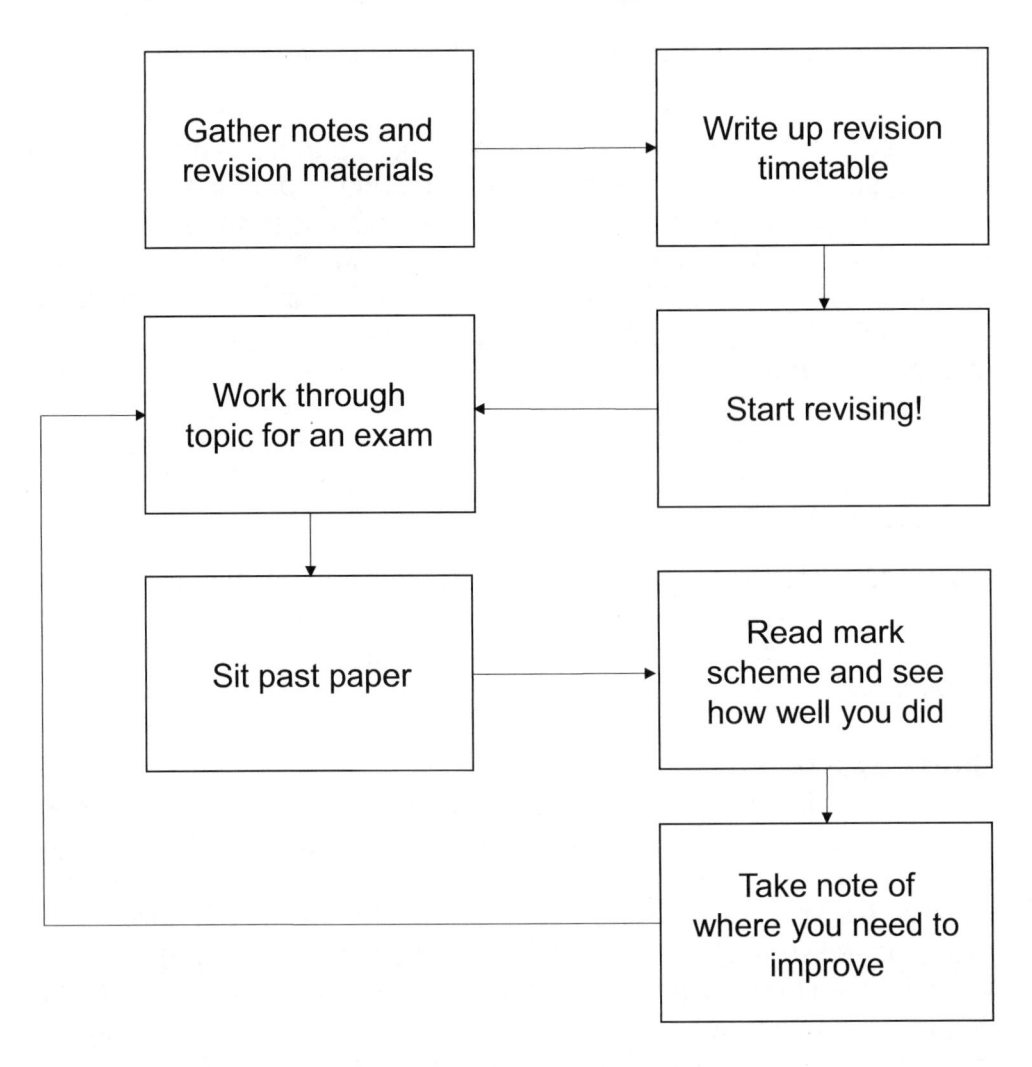

```
Gather notes and          →    Write up revision
revision materials              timetable
                                     ↓
Work through              ←    Start revising!
topic for an exam
      ↓
Sit past paper            →    Read mark
                                scheme and see
                                how well you did
                                     ↓
                               Take note of
                               where you need to
                               improve
```

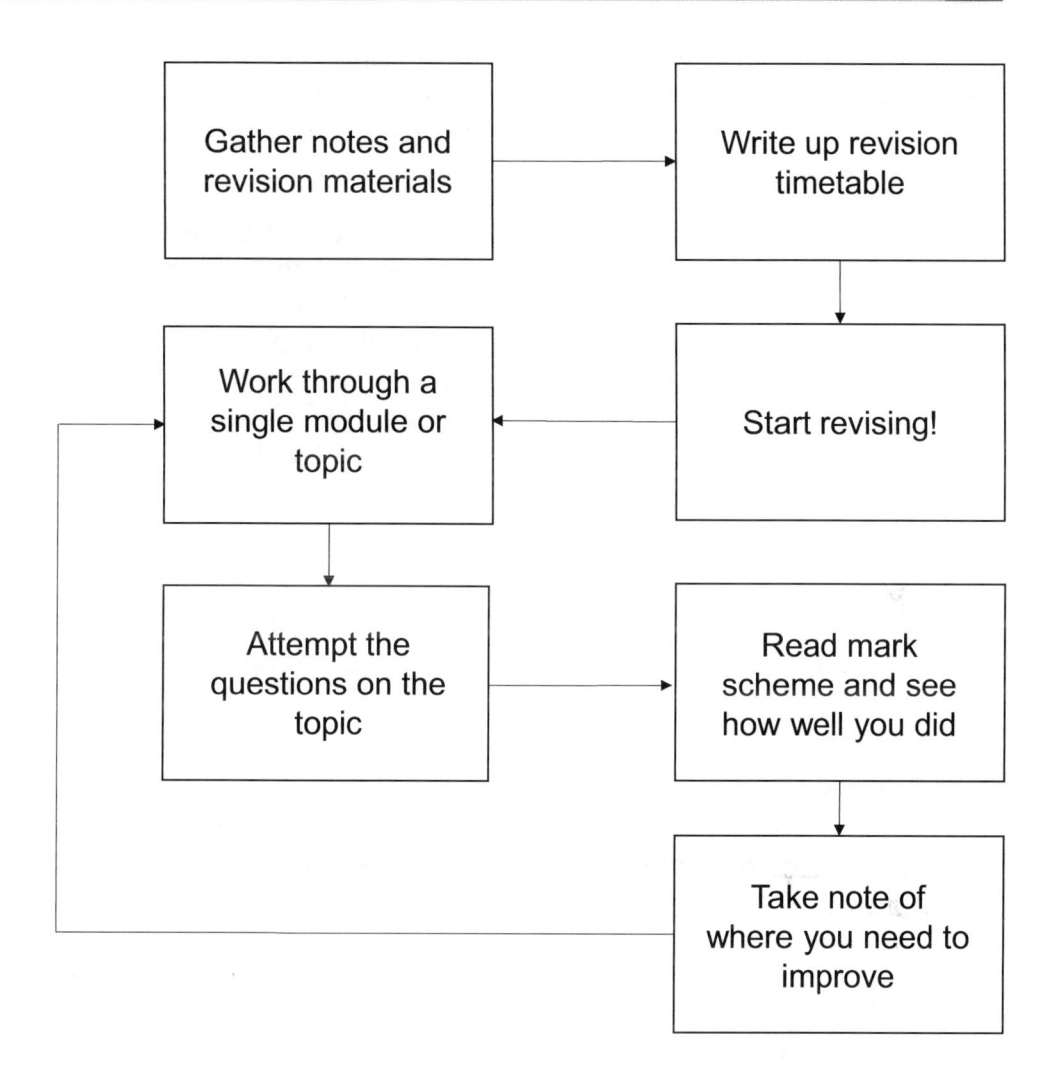

```
Gather notes and     →    Write up revision
revision materials        timetable
                               ↓
Work through a       ←    Start revising!
single module or
topic
    ↓
Attempt the          →    Read mark
questions on the          scheme and see
topic                     how well you did
                               ↓
                          Take note of
                          where you need to
                          improve
```
(arrow from "Take note of where you need to improve" back to "Work through a single module or topic")

Mark Schemes

Once you've done some practice papers, you'll want to know how well you've done. As we've mentioned previously, mock papers show you what you need to remember, what you know and what you need to improve on. However, sitting the paper is only half of the story. You'll also need to use a mark scheme to figure out what you do and don't know.

What are mark schemes?

Mark schemes are papers which examiners use when marking your exam. In the case of past papers, the mark schemes are the same ones which official GCSE examiners would use to mark your exams.

So, they're the most accurate source for answers. Depending on the exam, a mark scheme will include different content. For example, science exams will often simply give the correct answers since the questions are either right or wrong.

However, answers to essays in English papers aren't as straightforward. For exams with plenty of essay questions, the examiner will have criteria that they will need to look for in order to figure out what the quality of your work is. This is reflected in the mark scheme with a detailed description of what a higher level essay will look like, and will compare it to other essays of all quality levels. This can make it difficult to mark your own essays, so having your teacher mark them is very useful.

Mark schemes and answer sections can usually be found in the same place where you downloaded the practice papers. Keep away from looking at the mark schemes until you've finished the papers – you don't want to spoil the tests – but have them ready to go.

What are the benefits of using mark schemes?
Exam Criteria – Essays

Mark schemes have uses beyond simply finding out whether you have the answers right or wrong. In fact, reading mark schemes can be useful even if you aren't sitting a past paper because they'll show you what type of answers that the examiners are looking for. This is especially the case in essay-based exams, such as English, as well as other exams which include essays, such as modern foreign languages, history and geography. You can use mark schemes to find out what criteria the examiners use to mark your exams, and then compare what you've written to see how well you've done. Have you mentioned the key information that's listed for each answer? Have you answered the questions clearly, using an appropriate structure? Have you checked your spelling? All of these are going to be picked up on in essay-based exams, but it's worth reading a mark scheme to see how much each of these aspects affect your grade.

Jumping Through Hoops and Keywords

The other useful aspect of mark schemes is that they'll reveal key phrases and terms that will automatically improve your grade if you include them. This is an example of GCSEs requiring you to "jump through hoops" in order to succeed. Even in the subjects where there are no true right or wrong answers, there are often vital ingredients which you need to make reference to in order to secure marks. For example, a science question may look like this:

> How do animals change their traits over time?

This question is clearly about evolution. You could answer it like this:

> Animals are born with some small mutations in their genes. If these animals with the mutation are able to breed, new traits such as larger ears or better camouflage on their fur may start to appear over time. If these traits are advantageous, the animals with these traits will continue to reproduce and pass on their genes, whilst those without the genes will struggle to survive. Eventually, this means that all those without the genes will have died out, and those with the trait will be all that's left.

This is an adequate explanation for everyday use. However, in the exam you might be expected to give the name of this process as well. Since there have been multiple theories of evolution throughout history, the examiners will be expecting you to show that you know this is called "natural selection" – the theory of evolution discovered and developed by Charles Darwin, which is accepted today.

Sometimes, a mark scheme will specify that certain words or phrases need to be included in the answer in order to get the maximum number of marks. In some cases, these words need to be included to get any marks at all. For the above answer, you would be better off answering it with the following:

> Animals are born with some small mutations in their genes. If these animals with the mutation are able to breed, new traits such as larger ears or better camouflage on their fur may start to appear over time. If these traits are advantageous, the animals with these traits will continue to reproduce and pass on their genes, whilst those without the genes will struggle to survive. Eventually, this means that all those without the genes will have died out, and those with the trait will be all that's left. This process is known as natural selection.

Adding this at the end of your answer makes it more likely that you'll secure more marks. Mark schemes are helpful here because reading them will reveal what kind of key words the examiners are looking for. Look through a few years' worth of mark schemes to see if there any patterns. Are there any words or phrases which pop up a lot? If so, then these are ones that are certainly worth remembering in case you need to call on them in the exam.

It can be incredibly frustrating to know what something is, and be able to describe it (like in the answer above) but not remember the exact name of it. To get around this problem, it's a good idea to use flashcards in revision – they help you associate key phrases with their meanings and examples.

Exact Breakdown of Marks

Mark schemes can also be used to get an exact breakdown of an answer. Using the same example, the answer may award a single mark for lots of different things. For this question, let's pretend that this answer is worth 4 marks.

> Animals are born with some small mutations in their genes. If these animals with the mutation are able to breed, new traits such as larger ears or better camouflage on their fur may start to appear over time. If these traits are advantageous, the animals with these traits will continue to reproduce and pass on their genes, whilst those without the genes will struggle to survive. Eventually, this means that all those without the genes will have died out, and those with the trait will be all that's left. This process is known as natural selection.

The mark scheme could award marks for the following:

- 1 mark for mentioning mutations in genes.
- 1 mark for discussing traits.
- 1 mark for including advantageous/disadvantageous traits.
- 1 mark for giving the name of the process – natural selection.

> <u>Animals are born with some small mutations in their genes</u>. If these animals with the mutation are able to breed, <u>new traits such as larger ears or better camouflage on their fur</u> may start to appear over time. <u>If these traits are advantageous, the animals with these traits will continue to reproduce and pass on their genes, whilst those without the genes will struggle to survive.</u> Eventually, this means that all those without the genes will have died out, and those with the trait will be all that's left. <u>This process is known as natural selection.</u>

So, the breakdown of marks tells you exactly what you need to include in your answer, which will give you an idea of what you need to remember for the exam. Bear in mind that you might need to know more than what's given in the mark schemes, since you could be faced with a question which tackles the same topic but from a slightly different angle.

This information in the mark scheme means you could focus your answer even more. You might notice that a lot of the example answer is not underlined, and these details might not be necessary in order to gain full marks. With the information in the mark scheme, we can simplify and focus our answer:

> Animals are born with some small mutations in their genes. If these animals breed, new traits such as larger ears or better camouflage on their fur may start to appear over time. If these traits are advantageous, the animals with these traits will continue to reproduce and pass on their genes, whilst those without the genes will struggle to survive. This process is known as natural selection.

So, we now have a much shorter answer, which will give us as many marks as the longer answer would. This saves time, allowing us to move onto other questions in the exam.

Giving Precise Answers

In an exam, you might be tempted to fire off everything you know about a topic all at once. While it's great that you've remembered lots of information, it's not always a good idea to write absolutely everything you know when answering a question. Instead, you should figure out exactly what the question is asking from you. In the above example, we included a lot of information that wasn't necessary to get full marks.

You should aim to be as precise as possible with your answer – get straight to the point in order to save time. Mark schemes are useful here because they'll show you what the examiners are looking for. You can figure out what's required to get full marks in a question, then focus on giving that as your answer. In an exam, every second is precious; the less time you spend on unnecessary information, the more time you have for harder questions or for double-checking your work at the end. Efficiency is a great skill to have when it comes to exams, and using mark schemes to hone your answers will help you achieve this.

As well as saving you time, working on giving precise answers can make you sound more confident when giving your answers. Too much information can come across as waffle. While this isn't so much of an issue at GCSE, it's good to get into the habit of avoiding waffle if you want to go on to A-Levels.

With all this said, it's important that you make sure you answer every question in an exam as fully as possible. If you aren't sure what to write in your answer, it's better to give more information than less.

Stress

What is stress?
Stress is an unpleasant sensation you feel when you're under too much pressure. It's a common feeling to have as a student, especially when studying for and sitting your GCSE exams. The pressure that you feel can sometimes grow to become too much to deal with, and can be bad for your physical and mental health, not just your GCSE performance.

Stress can be the result of several different worries about your GCSEs. Worries can include:

- Will I get the grades I want/need?
- Have I revised enough?
- Have I left it too late to start revising?
- What will my family and friends think of me if I don't do well?
- What if bad questions show up in my exam?
- What if I oversleep and miss my exam?
- What if I get into the exam hall and forget everything?

Rest assured that, no matter what you're worried about in the run-up to your exams, thousands of other students have felt similar things. It's quite normal to feel a bit stressed during the exam period. However, it's important to keep these pressures in check, and prevent stress from harming you or your chances of acing your GCSEs. The rest of this section will be devoted to discussing stress, and will hopefully give you some advice on how to manage and prevent it.

How do I know if I'm feeling exam stress?

It can be difficult to know if you're stressed or not. Some people are genuinely stressed, but dismiss it as normal – perhaps because they do not know any different. If you're feeling stressed at all, it's important to identify it and make steps against it before stress becomes too much to handle.

The symptoms of stress occur because, when the body is under pressure, it releases hormones which trigger 'fight or flight' responses in the body. In prehistoric times, these symptoms may have proven useful for preparing the body to protect itself from a threat, or be able to run away quickly. Nowadays, we aren't particularly worried about fighting or escaping from wild animals, so the symptoms of stress aren't particularly helpful.

Stress has both emotional and physical symptoms. If you have any of the following symptoms, and feel unable to cope, then you might be stressed:

Emotional Symptoms	Physical Symptoms
Low self-esteem	Trouble sleeping
Anxiety	Sweating
Constant worrying	Loss of appetite
Short temper	Loss of concentration
	Headaches
	Dizziness

Whether you think you feel these symptoms or not, keep reading to find some methods for preventing stress, and some ways to reduce the stress that you may already have.

How can I prevent exam stress?

First of all, remember that exam stress is completely normal for students sitting their GCSEs. Your GCSEs are very important, and if you're feeling stressed about them it at least shows that you recognise their significance. While stress definitely isn't a good thing, the bright side of it is that you and your body are aware of how important your

GCSEs are. Now what's needed is to keep your stress levels down so you can operate at peak performance, and more importantly stay healthy in body and mind!

This section will cover the "dos" and "don'ts" for dealing with exam stress, both during revision and the exams themselves.

DO...

Start revision early. This might seem obvious by now, but starting your revision earlier in the year is one of the best ways to avoid stress. The more time you have, the less you need to do each day. This gives you more free time, and also allows you to make use of extra time to do other revision activities such as practice papers.

Have a countdown to the end of your exams. Buy a calendar and make note of all your exam dates. Tick days off as they go by, and stay focused on the end. Staying aware of the end point of your exams will remind you that there's life after your GCSEs. There is light at the end of the tunnel.

Listen to your body. At times, you might feel like an unstoppable machine, speeding through revision. During this period, it can be tempting to ignore your bodily needs and soldier on. Likewise, when you're worried about not finishing your revision in time for the exam, it seems like a good idea to stay up all night to make up lost time. Whether you're ignoring your body because you're doing well or poorly, it isn't advisable to do so. You can't function properly without food, water and sleep, so remember to take the breaks in your revision to do these things. That way, when you come back to revising, your study sessions will be more valuable because you're able to focus harder.

Forget about the exam once it's over. It's likely that you'll have more than one exam. You might even have multiple exams on consecutive days, or even on the same day. So, it's important not to linger on an exam once you've finished it. As soon as the exam ends, you have permission to forget about it entirely. Try and avoid talking to others about details of the exam, because it might give you second thoughts about what you wrote in yours. There's no use worrying now since there's no way of changing what you've written. Stay confident and move on to the next exam.

Remember that exams aren't the be-all and end-all. As we've already mentioned, life won't end if you don't get top marks in an exam. You might be disappointed by your grade, but remember that life goes on and your exam results won't ruin your life. What's just as important is a confident and prepared attitude, so even if you don't do as well as you'd hoped to, you should focus on moving forward, learning from your mistakes, and enjoying life.

Ask others for support. No person is an island, and everyone occasionally needs someone else to help them through tough times. Exams can be difficult, and a lot of pressure is put on students taking their GCSEs. When the going gets tough, don't be afraid to talk to your friends and family. Find people you trust and talk to them about your worries. Sometimes, just talking about things can make you feel calmer, even if you don't figure out any solutions. More often than not, your worries will be amplified by the general worry of exams, and so talking through your problems and rationalising them can be a form of therapy. You might find that your worries are just the result of paranoia, and aren't grounded in reality.

DON'T...

Don't rely on online forums. The internet can be an excellent place to find information and techniques for studying. You have access to plenty of specific advice on a range of subjects, and this can supplement your work in the classroom and your revision at home. However, not all resources are useful, and not all environments on the internet are good for your wellbeing. Some exam-focused chatrooms and forums can do more harm than good. You may come across people who are arrogant about the work that they've done, trying to make you feel worse about your studies as a result. Make use of the internet when it comes to your GCSEs, but try not to linger in places that won't make you feel better about your own studies.

Don't pay attention to how much revision others are doing. You'll likely find classmates who are all too willing to let you know how much revision they're doing, and how well their revision is going. These people are probably having a really hard time with their revision, and are just looking for a way to feel better about themselves. If you need to, ignore these people until your exams are over, and instead spend your free time with people who don't stress you out as much.

Don't get lazy because your friend has done less revision than you. Just as you'll probably come across someone who's apparently done a lot of revision, you probably have a friend or classmate who has apparently done no revision at all, or very little. While they might be telling the truth, it's also possible that they've actually done quite a lot of revision and they claim to have done little in order to look cool. It's tempting to get lazy about your revision because there's someone else who's done less, but remember that exams aren't about how well others are doing: it's about how well **you** are doing. In turn, this could lead to stress as you realise that you haven't done enough just before the exam. Make sure that you avoid getting lazy with your revision, and this will be far less likely to happen.

Don't set goals you can't meet. Always remember that there's only so much that you can do each day when it comes to revision. If you've put together a revision timetable then this shouldn't be a problem, but double-check how much work you've allotted for each day. During the revision period, take note of how much you're doing each day, and adjust your timetable based on this. For example, if you're finding that 10 topics is far too many, try reducing it to 7 or 8. Likewise, if you're able to do loads more than 5, experiment and see how many topics you get through in one day. The aim of this is to finish each day satisfied that you did everything you can, and that everything is completed. This should work towards preventing exam stress.

Don't panic about your exam timetable. Occasionally, you might not meet all of your goals for the day. While this isn't a good thing, you need to remember that you always have the next day to cover what you failed to achieve the day before. At the end of your revision for the day, you should try and put yourself in the mindset that everything is fine – meaning that you can relax and get some quality sleep.

Don't rely on caffeine or other stimulants. Caffeine will affect your concentration and sleep-patterns. If you become dependent on it, you'll find yourself unable to perform properly without it, which could lead to uncomfortable and unproductive revision sessions. This could cause stress over time, as you require a certain chemical in your body in order to feel ready to study or sit an exam. In addition, interrupting your sleeping-pattern can make you feel tired during your study time, and can cause stress in general. Do yourself a favour and keep away from the caffeine during the exam period.

Advice for Parents

Stress is felt amongst most students sitting their GCSEs. While it's normal to be slightly anxious about exams, you should keep an eye on how your child is behaving. As a teenager, your child may be quite defensive or quiet about their feelings towards exams, but if you see any of the symptoms listed earlier in this section, you should consider helping them. Here are a few of the ways in which you can help your child avoid feeling stressed during their exam period:

- **Make sure that they know you're happy to talk with them about their worries.** You don't need to pester your child, but if you notice that they're stressed, reminding them that they can talk to you whenever might convince them to open up a bit and talk. This could help them relieve lots of built-up stress.

- **Set time aside to talk to them if necessary.** Don't just let your child know that you're there to talk to, make sure that you're available at relatively short notice. This might not be possible during your own working hours, but while you're not at work, be ready to stop what you're doing and chat with your child. They'll really appreciate you being able to talk whenever they need you.

- **Respect their free time.** Teenagers hate being nagged to do things, especially revision. You need to make sure that they're actually working, but you also need to respect their free time and not interrupt them. One way to fix this is to ask for a copy of your child's revision timetable so that you know when they should be working and when they will be taking a break. This means that you know not to disrupt their breaks or free time by asking them whether they should be working or not. Your child will appreciate this since it allows them to relax after a hard day of revision.

- **Give your child what they need to succeed.** Make sure your child has good food to help them study and prevent stress. Ask them if there's anything in particular that they feel is necessary in order for them to do well, and help them in any way you can.

Conclusion

In many ways, exams are incredibly cruel, and can be very harsh. Just remember that almost everyone that you know has done GCSE exams before you, and people know what you are going through. In this chapter, you've been given lots of tips for coping with revision, as well as how to make sure that you are operating at peak performance during the exam itself.

However, if there's absolutely one thing that you must take away from this, it's that exams aren't the be-all and end-all in your life. They're certainly important, and you should take them seriously, but don't let yourself become distraught over worries about exams, or results which weren't as high as you might have hoped. There's much more to life than your GCSEs.

A FEW FINAL WORDS...

You have now reached the end of your guide for GCSE Religious Studies, and no doubt you feel more prepared to tackle your GCSE examination. We hope you have found this guide an invaluable insight into the test, and understand the expectations regarding your assessment.

For any type of test, we believe there are a few things to remember in order to better your chances and increase your overall performance.

REMEMBER – THE THREE Ps!

1. **Preparation.** This may seem relatively obvious, but you will be surprised by how many people fail their assessment because they lacked preparation and knowledge regarding their test. You want to do your utmost to guarantee the best possible chance of succeeding. Be sure to conduct as much preparation prior to your assessment to ensure you are fully aware and 100% prepared to complete the test successfully. Not only will practising guarantee to better your chances of successfully passing, but it will also make you feel at ease by providing you with knowledge and know-how to pass your Religious Studies GCSE.

2. **Perseverance.** You are far more likely to succeed at something if you continuously set out to achieve it. Everybody comes across times whereby they are setback or find obstacles in the way of their goals. The important thing to remember when this happens, is to use those setbacks and obstacles as a way of progressing. It is what you do with your past experiences that helps to determine your success in the future. If you fail at something, consider 'why' you have failed. This will allow you to improve and enhance your performance for next time.

3. **Performance.** Your performance will determine whether or not you are likely to succeed. Attributes that are often associated with performance are *self-belief, motivation* and *commitment*. Self-belief is important for anything you do in life. It allows you to recognise your own abilities and skills and believe that you can do well. Believing that you can do well is half the battle! Being fully motivated and committed is often difficult for some people, but we can assure you that, nothing is gained without hard work and determination. If you want to succeed, you will need to put in that extra time and hard work!

Good luck with your Religious Studies GCSE. We wish you the best of luck with all your future endeavours!

The How2Become Team

WANT FURTHER GUIDANCE FOR YOUR GCSEs?

CHECK OUT OUR OTHER GCSE GUIDES:

How2Become have created other FANTASTIC guides to help you prepare for a range of subjects at GCSE level:

FOR MORE INFORMATION ON OUR GCSE GUIDES, PLEASE CHECK OUT THE FOLLOWING:

WWW.HOW2BECOME.COM

NEED TO TAKE YOUR REVISION SKILLS TO THE NEXT LEVEL?

CHECK OUT OUR OTHER REVISION GUIDES:

- GCSE FRENCH IS EASY
- GCSE SPANISH IS EASY
- PASS YOUR A-LEVELS WITH A*s
- HOW TO STUDY: ACE YOUR GRADES
- ESSENTIAL WRITING TIPS
- HOW TO BE CRITICAL
- 24-HOURS TO A FIRST-CLASS ESSAY
- QUICK-FIRE MATHS
- ACE YOUR TIME MANAGEMENT
- IMPROVING YOUR MEMORY
- CONSTRUCTING YOUR ARGUMENT
- HOW TO STUDY WITH DYSLEXIA
- UNIVERSITY SURVIVAL POCKETBOOK

FOR MORE INFORMATION ON OUR REVISION GUIDES, PLEASE CHECK OUT THE FOLLOWING:

WWW.HOW2BECOME.COM

Get Access To

FREE

GCSE Resources

www.MyEducationalTests.co.uk